Clive Gregory's

FOUNDATIO
COURSE

for

BASS GUITAR

"The Essential Grounding In All Aspects Of Bass Playing".

Written by Clive Gregory during the late autumn of 1996. All music
examples specially composed for the project.

Edited by: J. Gregory

Assistant editor: G. Ellwood

Photographs by Michael Pearse

Artwork and design by Clive Gregory

Text and music typeset by R & C Gregory Publishing Limited

Special thanks to: Rubiah Gregory, Peter Wall, Michael Pearse, Graham
Mitchell, Ben Cooper, Mike Riley and Dan at Pulse and everyone at Colourscope
without whom this series of books would never have been possible.

First Edition published 1996 ISBN 1 901690 00 8
2nd impression, perfect bound, published 1997

Published by
R & C Gregory Publishing Limited

Suite 7, Unit 6, Beckenham Business Centre, Cricket Lane, Kent. BR3 1LB.

ISBN 1 901690 20 2

Printed by CS PRINT & DISPLAY Limited, Croydon, England.

This book is dedicated to my wife, Kobbi for her unwavering support during this project. Also to my parents for a lifetime of support.

The book is also dedicated to all of my students, past and present without whom this book would not have been possible.

Clive Gregory started teaching Bass in 1980. Over the past sixteen years he has taught many hundreds of bass players, from beginners to session players.

As a working professional over 19 years he has played in a great many bands of every conceivable type and has played on TV, TV jingles, radio jingles, and on BBC radio broadcasts.

His considerable knowledge and experience as bass player and dedicated teacher has at last been made available to a wider audience through his first book. The Foundation Course is the first in a planned series of publications and is typical of his thorough approach to the subject. It reflects his understanding of the problems faced by beginners to music and by more experienced bass players - nothing is assumed, everything is patiently explained.

CONTENTS

Introduction

Welcome to Clive Gregory's Foundation Course for Bass Guitar. This book is intended as a complete instruction guide to playing bass from beginner right up to near professional level. I always describe this as competence level. On completion of this foundation course you will have the basic skills and knowledge to understand all the major processes that make up bass playing today. I have placed great stress, as I do when teaching one to one, on understanding the application of a particular subject in the real world of bass playing.

The book is laid out in such a way that it will appeal equally to absolute beginners as much as experienced players looking to revise areas of weakness in their playing or learning a new subject, such as sight-reading.

The book is grouped into 5 main topics;

- Technique
- Musicianship
- Playing & reading
- Improvisation and composition
- Ear training (pitch & rhythm)

You can use the book to take you from a complete beginner to a working bass player. It can also be used as a top quality revision course for more experienced bass players who wish to learn a new subject and/or improve their standard of musicianship. For beginners, completion of this book will give you all the basic knowledge and skill you need to join a quality band. This means a band that is playing live and perhaps doing some demo recording. In this book the topics are broken down into 6 target periods. These targets are intended to represent approximately 1 months study. Of course everyone learns at a different rate so this is purely a guideline. You will usually find that some topics are easier to grasp than others - but hopefully you understand the concept of the book.

Throughout this book you will come across information boxes like this one. Rather than give a list of great Bass Players, great records, great tracks, great bass guitars etc. at the end, I have decided to use boxes like this to give a brief description of one Bass Player or record of significance to Bass Players

My favourite Bass is my Status series 2000 which I've owned since 1985. This is the bass that you will see featured in the photographs. The bass is made entirely from carbon fibre, for great strength and sustain (and an interesting appearance). The electrics are very versatile, and the balance of the instrument is perfect. If you've got £1,300 - buy one.

How To Use This Book

The Approach For Beginners:

If you have just bought a bass for the first time and are perhaps taking your first steps exploring music in general then you really need to follow the book through step by step. Music and Bass Guitar study is a huge undertaking. There is a great deal of knowledge to attain and many skills to acquire. If you have serious ambitions it is worth remembering that professional musicianship is a high pressure business. If your studies have not been thorough, you are likely to crack under the strain. This said, learning bass should be masses of fun, and while you need to work hard, you should never punish yourself if the going gets tough, and never allow problems to get you down. Within reason, if your practice is getting bogged down at any time then move on to the next subject, or put a record on for some inspiration. For players of all abilities please read the chapter "In the beginning", as it is in this chapter that I introduce all the major concepts of technique and many of the aims and attitudes of bass playing. You will probably find yourself referring back to this chapter frequently when using this book. Then move onto the first target period - Target 1. Concentrate on each topic within this section of the book. Try and resist the temptation to move on to the 2nd target of a particular topic until every topic has been thoroughly understood. The point about this is that studying music and bass guitar is like constructing a huge jigsaw; there are many pieces which must fit together before you have a complete picture. For example suppose you find technique easy and fascinating and practise exercises and scales all day, so that you can play fast all over the fingerboard, you will not find this impresses many other musicians, because they will expect you to be able to accompany their songs, communicate with them and **play incredibly good time.**

So every subject needs to be in balance. This requires more patience and discipline but will achieve much more in the long run. Also try to remember that most people you listen to and admire, have been playing for many years and have worked extremely hard to achieve their goals. You cannot become a good bass player in days or weeks. However, you can become very competent in a matter of a few months. It is not unknown for some people to be able to make a living after only playing for a year or two. This is why I've very carefully structured this course so that each target (all topics) represents roughly 1 months study.

The Approach For More Experienced Players.

Firstly read the above paragraphs on the approach for beginners because if you are not strong in all departments of playing bass you may wish to take the approach outlined for beginners.

Assuming you are happy with some aspects of your playing and have bought this book to improve other aspects, that you're not so good at, then the book can also be used to go through by the topic, rather than from target to target. Let's assume that you are not a reader and want to work on this aspect. Firstly, read the chapter "In The Beginning", as this may include important comments about the approach and attitudes towards reading music. Then find Target 1, Playing and Reading. Looking at the title you may think this is two topics in one, which in a way it is, however, if you are studying how to read music you will of course need pieces of music to play, whilst reading, and so you should cover every aspect you find in this section.

Occasionally you may be referred to another section of the book. Please follow these referrals as they will be relevant to your current study. For example when studying reading music, you may be referred to the ear-training section where more specific rhythm exercises are contained.

In General

Rather than include boring discography's at the end of the book I have put boxes (see page 1) throughout the book highlighting either artists or records that have been inspirations to myself, or important milestones in bass guitar history, or references to guitar makers and types of bass guitar etc. I am hoping that you are more likely to remember names of great bass players this way as they'll be introduced one by one over a period of time.

In The Beginning - Technique

As a student of music and bass guitar in particular, you will find some aspects come naturally and other aspects are seemingly impossible. Some people's hands seem to be naturally made for bass playing whereas others seem at first to be completely useless. Some people can apparently pick up a tune as easily as reading the headline in a newspaper whereas others feel that they are completely tone deaf. The point to remember here is that music is like a large jigsaw made up of many pieces and you need all of the pieces to become a good musician and bass player. Take heart from the fact that if you're finding one subject difficult when your friends find it easy, that almost certainly there will be a subject which you find easy and they find impossible. You also need to try and counter the natural instinct to hide from (or not practice) that which you find difficult, and avoid over-practising those subjects that come naturally. It is important that you enjoy your studies but music is a huge subject and if you refuse to work when the going gets tough you will not progress very far.

Left hand technique - aims and objectives

The left hand needs to be able to cover the maximum possible area as quickly and as quietly as possible. A good left hand technique is logically a way of playing that allows for this objective. You will give yourself more creative options if you work at developing a good technique. A good technique will involve developing a good, even stretch from the first finger to the fourth with an equal spread between the

fingers. You will need to have strength and balance in the arm so that the hand is supported. Note that if you try and support the hand by hanging onto, or gripping the neck too tightly, your freedom of movement will be considerably reduced. Your fingers need to develop the correct shape. This is with all joints curved, if only slightly. You need to avoid any 'locked' joints as they will stiffen up the hand and slow you down. The fingers must learn to find the lightest possible touch as pressing down too hard will both slow you down and tire you much more quickly. The fingers need to find the most efficient method of pressing the strings down so that the string makes contact with the fret. If this is not done then you will find yourself pressing over hard to make the note clean. Overall, movement in the left hand should be smooth and fluent. Remember you develop good technique over months and years of playing so that your creative options are maximised and because you want to play with ease, fluency and efficiency.

Developing good left hand technique begins with good posture and adjustment of the strap to support the instrument at the correct height. The height you set the bass is controversial because of the different image this conveys. Typically the more rebellious your image, the lower the bass (wrapped around the knees is not uncommon), whereas with the bass high on the chest a very 'muso' image is conveyed. My advice to my students has always been to set the height in your practice sessions to the correct height for your hands and arms. This is measured by ensuring that your left forearm is just pointing upwards from the elbow when you place your hand on the fingerboard. This is not just so that your hand will be in the most effective place but also to ensure that you reduce any risk of injury. It is easier than you might think to damage your hands, sometimes permanently, by adopting the wrong technique. One possible injury is tendinitis which can be caused by playing with the wrist bent to its maximum for a long period of time. By ensuring that your forearm is always pointing upwards you minimise the risk of this type of injury.

By now you will hopefully be sitting with your back straight and with your forearm pointing slightly upwards towards the neck of the bass. Before you attempt to get your fingers working correctly you need to understand the role of your upper arm and shoulder. The upper arm should try to take all of the weight of the forearm and hand. Although when you lift your arm up from your side it is not obviously tiring, holding your arm in this position for several minutes certainly is. Start by holding the arm in this position, without actually touching the bass, for three minutes. This should not be too difficult, however, it should be long enough for you to appreciate which muscles are being put under strain. This will enable you to notice when the arm is getting slack and make it easier to correct.

The thumb of the left hand is placed approximately in the centre of the back of the neck and should lie more or less under the 2nd finger of the left hand. The thumb's job is not to enable the fingers to grip the

neck but is to balance the hand and facilitate ease of movement from one string to the next. Practice this movement first of all; with the thumb in position place the fingers very roughly over the strings and move the hand from the 'G' string to the 'E' string. Do this by pivoting around the thumb. Keep the ball of the thumb in the same place on the back of the neck and watch the forearm moving forward and backward from the elbow, with the wrist moving from almost completely bent, when your fingers are over the 'E' string, to a very relaxed curve when your fingers are over the 'G' string.

The fingers are clearly at the sharp end of left hand technique, but don't try and skip the above, as without good support and balance of the hand you will find it very difficult to make your fingers work efficiently. The first point to establish is that you want to try and develop a finger per fret technique. Most bass players adopt this technique as it logically gives the best possible access to the largest number of notes. Start off by putting your first finger just behind the 5th fret on the A (3rd) string. Next put your 2nd finger just behind the 6th fret of the A string. Slightly more difficult at first is to put your 3rd finger just behind

the 7th fret and your 4th finger just behind the 8th fret. You will have realised by now that the best place to 'connect' with a note is to put your finger just behind the fret you want the string to make contact with. Placing the finger here means that you can get away with much less pressure than placing your finger further back, say right in the middle of two frets. (Another benefit of playing accurately right behind the frets is that should you ever decide to take up fretless bass, you will have a technique ready made for that particular instrument.) Next look at the shape of your fingers, you probably have a mixture of shapes depending on how easy you are finding it to get your fingers right behind the frets. They should all be curved and pressing the string down with the tips of the fingers. Also take another look at the thumb, is it still lying roughly under the 2nd finger on the centre of the back of the neck. (If you have quite small hands, don't be afraid to push the thumb further towards the 'G' string side of the neck to enable you to get your fingers into position.) The shape to aim for is that each finger is making contact with the string at the tip of the finger. This is not so that your hand looks neat, although it should do, but because your finger will be hardest at this point, you are using the bone of the finger to make contact with the string. If you play with the fingers too flat across the fingerboard then you have to press through much more flesh to make contact with the string. This will in turn mean that you have to press much harder, slowing you down and tiring you more quickly. Also the fingers should be evenly curved, don't allow any joint to be straight and locked. A locked joint has to be unlocked before it can be moved, making it a very cumbersome tool.

SUMMARY: The most important part of left hand development is patience. You will not achieve a perfect technique overnight, it will take days to feel even a little bit comfortable, weeks to feel easy and possibly months to feel totally natural. Good technique has not evolved from people taking the easy route it has come about by trial and error and by having the vision to look at what you want the hand to be able to do in a few months, even a few years time and developing a technique to deal with future problems and ambitions.

Also don't push too fast. You need to take care of your hands, make sure that you don't strain the muscles, especially in the thumb. However, you do need to be determined. For some people good technique is not easy, some people's hands are less well made for bass playing than others but if you do find it difficult at first, persevere because in 17 years of teaching hundreds of bass players I cannot think of anyone who has not been able to overcome physical weaknesses in the hand.

Right Hand Technique - Main aims

You are probably thinking that the right hand is the less important and less interesting hand of the two. However, bass players only succeed if they can deliver a good sound in perfect time. Both timing and sound are delivered by the right hand. There are many styles that are employed by bass players for striking the strings and whatever style(s) you eventually settle on, you have to work hard to achieve a good sound with impeccable timing. The point I'm trying to make is that as far as other people are concerned, the people that hire you or ask you to join their band etc., what is delivered by your right hand is 90% of their concern. Of course we all want inventive bass lines that are interesting to play, both for our own pleasure and for the audience, but a great bass player can play two or three simple notes in a phrase and make the whole audience smile, whereas a bass player without the ability to deliver a good groove will drive an audience away in no time at all. (I will discuss groove in more detail later but for now think of it as the combination of consistently good sound and timing).

Fingerstyle;

The most common approach to the right hand is alternating the index and middle fingers. Some bass players incorporate the 3rd finger and/or the thumb but for now we'll concentrate on the index and middle finger approach. Initially, it is necessary to develop a technique that can act as a benchmark for all right hand work. Once you have established this benchmark you can then 'break the rules' to gradually achieve a wider range of sounds and tonal possibilities.

Firstly, you need to learn to support the hand. As with left hand technique this begins at the shoulder and upper arm. Position the right hand so that the index and middle fingers are resting against the 'G' string. The wrist should be elevated so that the fingers are at about a 45° angle to the strings. The thumb should be resting up against the 'E' string, although place the tip of the thumb on the body of the bass. If your hands are large, you may find that you need to place the tip of the thumb an inch or so away from the 'E' string. (Don't worry about damping the strings just yet - getting the balance of the hand correct is the priority for now.)

With the middle finger resting on the string build up some pressure and finally force the finger 'through' the string. The force of the finger movement should be such that the middle finger finds itself firmly against the 'D' string. Next do the same with the index finger. At first don't try and play too rapidly, concentrate on getting the 'feel' right.

With finger-style playing you need to play quite firmly. This is to give each note a definite attack or strong beginning. Even a lot of experienced bass players don't realise just how hard they play as this has usually evolved. However, if you are a beginner it will do you no harm to play harder than might be necessary. I have only ever known about 2 students who played too hard and it is usually easier to learn to relax later than to try and increase the force of playing once you are set in your ways. Other benefits to playing hard are that you will increase your available dynamic range (loud to soft). You will produce a sound with more overtones, enabling you to achieve a wider range of sounds both acoustically and electronically. You will also find it easier to cut through the rest of the band. If you practise slightly harder than you intend playing, you will have good stamina.

Musicianship

If you are a beginner to music you might be forgiven for thinking that music theory is a subject to avoid. I have entitled the subject musicianship in the hope that you'll realise that being a good musician requires knowledge as well as technical skill. Knowledge about how music is put together enables you to develop more ideas - more quickly. Anyone can have a tape of a new song and after a day or two of trial and error come up with a bass part that sounds acceptable. However, I would expect to have several ideas for a bass part upon first listening to a song. As a professional player I might be expected to hear a song or composition for the first time, and within a few minutes be recording a finished bass line. Without a thorough musical knowledge this would not be possible.

Even if you have no intention of becoming a professional bass player, the same importance to speed and ease of working can be applied to a normal band situation. Musicians like to work with bass players that know what they are doing, and bass players that have ten ideas rather than one. It is the purpose of this book to concentrate on areas of knowledge that are of real practical value. It definitely is not my intention to give example after example of musical situations that you may never encounter, even as a working professional. I have always tried to keep the use of musical jargon to a minimum, any jargon that is used you can be sure is in common usage by many working musicians.

This section will help you to understand how music is put together. The good news here is that almost all music is put together in the same way. Punk and grunge music is put together using the same 'rules' and techniques as classical music. In other words, we as 20th century musicians can benefit from all of the work that has been done over the past four or five hundred years by thousands of musicians and composers. It is not important that only a very small proportion of those people knew what a bass guitar was, what matters is that they all created music.

Musical knowledge is useful.

One of my problems over the years has been to persuade people, who basically want to play rock and roll and have a wild and rebellious image, that musical knowledge is relevant to them. As with anything in life, if your can use your brain to achieve your goals then you're likely to get there a lot faster and the result is likely to be very much better. Even if you start out as a wild rocker you may find yourself gradually being seduced by the challenges of jazz playing. As you progress in music the challenges are less and less technical and more and more intellectual. A very important point before you begin your studies in this section, is that musical knowledge or intellect is only ever going to be valuable to you if you learn thoroughly. You have to hold information in your sub-conscious so that you act instinctively on it. Anything less than this and you'll find your brain works too slowly to make your knowledge advantageous. Musicians often fall into the trap of thinking that learning music theory will help them to play, without realising that it will only help them when it is thoroughly absorbed. When playing music things happen very fast, you can't consciously work out the notes in a chord as you get to it because by the time you've figured it out, the rest of the band will have finished the entire verse.

It does take time to get your knowledge to this point. What you have to do is to be working with the information on a regular basis. Constantly trying to improve the depth of your knowledge. In this book there is nothing fanciful about the ideas presented, the information is practical and useful day in day out. If you are a beginner reading this then you are at an advantage from the more advanced player that has perhaps seen the error of omitting theory or knowledge from their studies. You can learn about how music is put together at the same time as you acquire your technical skills.

Ear Training

Having a 'good ear' is something that many people contemplating studying music expect to have naturally. It is true that some people have a natural aptitude towards hearing musical sound. One thing is certain, whether you have or have not got a good ear to start with, in order to become an effective musician you will need to 'train' your hearing. If you don't feel confident about your hearing then the purpose of this book is to help change that.

As musicians, we need to be able to recognise sound in two principal areas; pitch and rhythm. For pitch recognition it is not usually necessary to be able to listen to a note, first thing in the morning - at random, and be able to say unhesitatingly that the note we're hearing is an 'A' or an 'E' etc.. This ability is known as perfect pitch, and while it has been proved that it can be learned, this ability seems to be the gift of a very few people. The attainment of perfect pitch is not within the scope of this book. In this book we will concentrate on how to recognise the difference in pitch between two notes. It is vital in music, that if we know the starting note, or the key of the music that we can follow the melody and chord progression of that music by ear. Knowing, by judging the difference between two notes what each note in turn must be. If you're having trouble identifying with this idea, then imagine that you're recording a new version of a famous song. You can very probably sing or hum the main tunes to this song quite naturally without any musical training. As a musician, playing bass guitar, you need to understand the tune you're singing in such a way that if required, you could immediately play it on the bass. If your understanding is good enough to enable you to do this, then you can say that you are 'hearing' the song correctly. It is logical that if this can be done for melody, then it can be done for harmony or chord progressions. The goal of this foundation course is to help develop your hearing to this extent. On completion of this book you should be able to hear common chord progressions and conventional melody with ease.

Rhythm needs to be understood by ear. Rhythmic variation is seemingly endless, yet for the most part the rhythms we hear, day in day out - used in records, are created by mixing 18 principal rhythm patterns. There are a great many more rhythms in existence than this, however, throughout most of this book we will concentrate on expertise in playing and hearing these rhythms and understanding how these basic rhythmic patterns can be responsible for so much variety in rhythm.

The goal of this book is to enable you to recognise immediately any rhythmic combination comprising the 18 principal rhythms.

Playing & Reading

Playing bass lines will be what it's all about for most people. Whether you're playing a part that you've composed yourself or a part made famous by one of the worlds' great bass players it is, of course, playing and performing that we all want to do. For the purposes of this book all bass lines have been specially composed to give examples of bass playing in line with the ability you're likely to have at that particular stage in your studies. It is not within the scope of this book to use lines by other bass players. Transcriptions of famous bass lines are becoming more widely available and should be acquired in addition to a tutorial course such as this. In the playing sections of the book I will be gearing most of my instruction towards how to *really* play. Most bass lines that you hear on records are rhythmically and melodically quite simple - of course there are tricky lines, even on some pop records - but the vast majority are technically quite easy. However, that doesn't mean that just anybody can walk into the studio and record these lines. The art of the musician is not so much in the physical playing of notes in the right order but the feeling that is put into the notes and playing in order to communicate with the audience. Music is an emotional experience. Whatever the style, we as musicians have to try and create a reaction in our audience, an emotional reaction. If you're into rock then you have to create a reaction of hard, even aggressive excitement. If you're playing soul then you're trying to make your audience feel either romantic or sexy. There are a number of ways that these emotional messages can be sent by musicians to the audience, the techniques of feel and groove will be discussed throughout the book. But always remember that music is the art of communication with an audience rather than a means of self-indulgent egotism. The following represents a summary of the main points to consider when trying to achieve feel and groove:

For the Bass Player it is how, rather than what, you play that really matters. A great bass player can make a few simple notes sound incredible. So what is 'a good groove' and how do you play with 'feel'?

A groove can best be described as the aim of the bass player, a riff or improvised bass part played with total consistency from start to finish. It is this consistency that all the bass players share, whatever their predominant style or background. It is consistency that is the most difficult skill to acquire as a musician. A combination of feel and time-keeping are the means with which to establish a groove. Time-keeping has to be precise, the main (usually 4/4) beat must be close to perfect, when dividing the beat into 8's, 12's or 16's the way each subdivision is played must match throughout the songs length. Eighth notes can be swung, by delaying the 2nd eighth note - bit by bit until you arrive in triple time, when logically you should refer to the sub-division as triplets or 12's. Swinging triplets (12's) means to delay the 2nd and 3rd notes of the triplet very slightly, and swinging 16's involves delaying the 2nd and 4th sixteenth notes in each beat. However you play a song, swung or in strict time, you must keep it consistent or the groove will be lost.

Feel, ultimately, should be simply a feeling, an emotion; elation, sadness, aggression etc. the closer you can get to the emotion of a song whilst you are playing it the better it will feel and sound and the better it will communicate to others. Being a musician is similar to being an actor in that you are often called upon to play a role (feel an emotion) at a moments notice. As with actors, the more genuine the feeling for the role you adopt, the more convincing the performance.

Technically, feel is produced by subtle combinations of tone-colour (timbre), accents and articulation of individual notes. Consistency is again vital, the degree to which you accent the first note of the bar, for example, must be constant.

Timbre: practise plucking a string, with the same finger at the same angle, starting near the bridge and listen to the tone change as you move slowly towards the neck. Now pick any spot within the playing area and pluck the string with the finger as flat onto the body of the bass as possible and gradually push the arm forward, changing the striking angle and continuing until the finger has curved round and is scooping the string upwards - again you should hear a very noticeable change of tone. Next appreciate **dynamics**, that is the range in volume possible on your instrument. It is achieved by plucking as softly as possible and gradually playing harder until you are plucking as hard as possible with the bass quite probably rattling from top to bottom - this is your dynamic range. You should practise and strive for as great a dynamic range as possible. You should now begin to see what is possible, infinite tonal possibilities, infinite variation in the strength of notes, from accented to normal to 'whispered'.

Next, you have control over the articulation of each note, that is, the precise length of a note. From full length, a note that sustains right up to the following note (stress), to a note played as short as possible (staccato).

Finally, you have special expressive tricks and possibilities that can be used to enhance your playing further. Snapping the string onto the frets (popping), dead (unpitched) notes, semi-muted and ghost notes, plucking with finger nails - really any way you can think of to make new sounds that will enhance the music.

So, if you can combine all these elements: • strong emotional feeling • time keeping • swing • timbre • dynamics • accents • articulation • special expressive tricks, and if you can maintain consistency in each element from beat 1 to the very end of a song, day in day out, then you'll be a successful bass player. Remember that an objective ear is a very important ally when studying this subject. Listen, really listen to your playing, record yourself and listen back, play the recordings to other people and get their opinion, listen to the bass masters, and always strive to make HOW YOU PLAY count.

Reading

Reading music is a subject that some people would rather not get involved with. I always try to persuade students to get into reading by comparing music to a foreign language. If you were living in another country, having to survive and work there, you would quickly come to the conclusion that you'd have to be able to speak the language. You would also soon feel isolated if you could only speak the language but were unable to read and write the language. Reading a language or music enables you to absorb much more information than you could by just speaking it. Your overall knowledge and confidence in the language would also be considerably enhanced, similarly with reading and writing music. Perhaps the best reason for learning to read music is that it's actually quite easy. Learning to read at sight, the ability to play immediately a piece of written music, is a more difficult subject, but as with all the other subjects that make up the musical jigsaw it helps the other pieces fit together and is itself helped by increasing your knowledge in other areas. There is also a knack or technique to sight reading. If you follow the instructions in the Playing and Reading sections of the book, there is no reason why you shouldn't be able to read quite well in a matter of months. The target of this book is to help take you to a sufficiently high standard to be able to start working as a reading musician.

(Reading will definitely increase your chances of getting work if you have the ambition to be a professional bass player.)

Improvisation & Composition

The ability to improvise is a complete mystery to many musicians. To a large extent it is made possible by having a good knowledge of how music is put together and having a well trained ear. It is quite a difficult subject only in that your knowledge of music and the bass needs to be thorough, therefore hard work is a better description than difficult. The improvisation sections of this book will concentrate on specific areas of knowledge for the subject. They will expect you to either know already or to study basic musicianship and theory elsewhere in the book. Composition is closely linked with improvisation as the knowledge required to do either is basically the same. At an early stage in your studies, your approach to composing a bass line where you've time to experiment and analyse, will be different to improvisation where the emphasis is on immediate performance.

In both improvisation and composition it is obviously impossible for me to give you creative ability. But I believe that we all are packed full of ideas, some good, some not so good and what I will endeavour to do is help you find the ideas that are bursting to get out of your system and into a bass line.

*   *   *

Tuning The Bass

It is important to ensure that you are perfectly in tune before you begin any work with the bass. It is just as important that you are perfectly in tune for practising as it is for a recording session or gig.

There are a lot of electronic tuners on the market, some are quite reasonably priced. I prefer chromatic tuners to the type where you select the string and then tune, however, they do tend to be the more expensive type. Although electronic tuners are useful for beginners and for taking with you on a gig or session you should learn how to tune by ear. It is often necessary to tune to a specific instrument that may not be capable of re-tuning, such as a grand piano at a venue. When working with others don't rely on your tuner being the same as the other musicians tuning. You will come across much better if you are prepared to tune to others should they request it. These circumstances require you to know how to tune the instrument by ear as well as just being a good musician and knowing your instrument.

You are never expected to be able to guess where to start (although I can usually tune fairly accurately as I know that the lowest note I can sing is about E flat. I tune the E string to this note and then sharpen by a semitone and then tune the rest of the bass to this). For now though go and buy a tuning fork which is very inexpensive - and should last a lifetime. This will, when struck ring a very accurate note which you can amplify either by standing on a resonating surface, like a tabletop, or by holding over your pickup. Try and buy a 'D' fork if you can find one, or else A (which is the most readily available tuning fork) will do fine.

At the very beginning use open strings to tune. It doesn't matter which string you tune first as long as all the other strings are tuned to this starting point. It does avoid confusion though if you begin with the G string. Tune this to your tuning fork. The open G string should then act as the standard for the other strings. Fret the 5th fret on the D string. This note should be exactly the same. If it is higher then slacken the machine head slowly and progressively until it is the same as the open G, obviously tighten the machine head if your D string is flat. (If you look at your fingerboard chart on page 12, you will notice that both these notes should sound mid G). Your D string is now in tune, so sound this open D whilst fretting the 5th fret of the A string, and tune. When the A string is in tune, repeat the process for the E string.

Take advantage of the phenomenon of 'beats' when tuning. Basically when two notes are played together that are slightly out of tune with one another, you get beats or pulses in the sound. If you are quite a long way out of tune these beats will be rapid and the sound will be quite jarring, if the two notes are almost in tune, the beat will be slow. When there is no beat, upon playing two notes together then these notes will be in tune. A good exercise to get used to the feel of your machine heads and how much they alter the pitch when you turn them is to try and sound both notes, while they are still ringing strongly slowly and progressively turn the machine head. Listen to the beats as you turn, if you were in tune to start with you should hear the speed of the beats increase, keep turning until the speed of the beats is so fast that it is almost impossible to hear it as beats, then turn slowly and progressively in the opposite direction, listen to the beats slow down and, as you come into perfect tune, stop.

You may quickly discover that turning the machine heads and fretting the 5th fret requires you to grow another arm or turn yourself into a contortionist. A better method is to use harmonics. Harmonics are obtained by lightly touching the string in specific places. It is beyond the scope of this book to go into any detail about harmonics and using them in playing, however you will find that you can get a harmonic easily by touching the string lightly over the 12th fret (Touch the string firmly, but ensure that the string does not actually move towards the fingerboard). When you can get a harmonic over the 12th fret, try over the 7th fret and then over the 5th. The first thing you'll notice about harmonics is that their pitch is a lot higher than normal notes. For most people this higher pitch is easier to hear clearly, and therefore better for tuning. If you take you finger off the string after you pluck with the right hand you will also notice that the harmonic keeps ringing. This is useful for tuning as you will be able to sound a note and then comfortably move your left hand to turn the machine head. Harmonics also enable you to hear the 'beats' more easily.

When using harmonics to tune use those harmonics that are over the 7th and 5th frets. The harmonics over the 7th fret correspond to the notes below them and so are (from E string to G string) B, E, A, D. Start by playing the D harmonic, which is over the 7th fret on the G string. Assuming that this note is in tune then play the harmonic over the 5th fret on the D string. Make sure that on each string you are playing that your fingers only touch the string at the point of playing the harmonic, as a second contact will dampen the harmonic. These two notes should be the same. If they are out of tune you will hear beats as you did with open string and 5th fret. Use the beats to tune accurately. Repeat the process of 7th to 5th fret harmonics for each string in turn.

The Bass Guitar - Overview

Bass Guitars are available in just about any shape and colour. They are built from a variety of materials, from inexpensive woods to the most exotic (and expensive) woods from around the world. High tech materials such as carbon fibre and aluminium. are also used either entirely or for the construction of the neck. Necks are sometimes bolted onto the body and other designs have the neck travelling through the body for the full length of the bass. There are innumerable designs for the bridge pieces and also for tuning. The original, and still most widely used tuning method, is by use of machine heads mounted on the headstock. More modern methods tune the bass at the tail piece end - this system is more stable. The electronics vary from the simplest tone filter to multiple switches, parametric equalisers or very high quality active electronics, allowing the player to cut or boost in the same way that is possible on a professional mixing desk.

It is only my intention to give you a brief tour of the bass on this page, when buying a bass you will find that for the most part you get what you pay for. My recommendation for beginners is to spend as little as possible until you have learned the basics. After this you will be much better at judging what is the right bass for you. Another tip when looking for a bass is to be sure of your priorities. You don't have to follow mine but I always judge a bass in this order:
BALANCE (you need of course to use a strap to fully judge this quality)
GENERAL FEEL OF THE INSTRUMENT WHEN PLAYING, ESPECIALLY THE NECK (width and depth vary greatly)
THE BOTTOM END SOUND (some basses just cannot produce good low notes, low G and F provide the best test, open E should be OK on most basses but is vitally important)
ACCOUSTIC SOUND (Playing unamplified reveals the true tone of the instrument and is a clue to the bass's ability to sustain)
ELECTRONICS (Simplicity of use with the widest possible range of sounds is my preference)
FUN FACTOR (difficult to explain, but you'll know when a bass has it)
APPEARANCE.

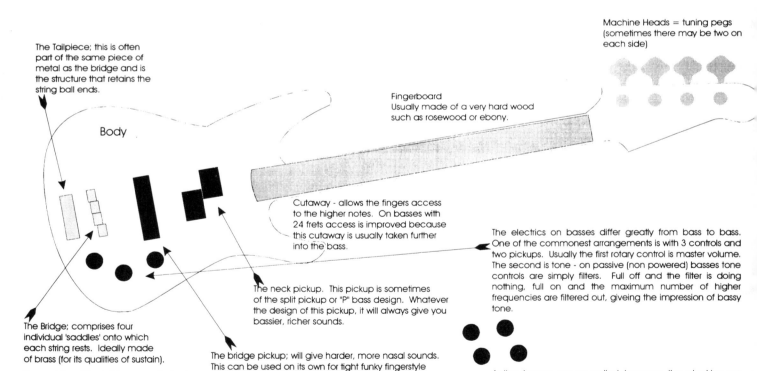

Machine Heads = tuning pegs (sometimes there may be two on each side)

The Tailpiece; this is often part of the same piece of metal as the bridge and is the structure that retains the string ball ends.

Fingerboard
Usually made of a very hard wood such as rosewood or ebony.

Body

Cutaway - allows the fingers access to the higher notes. On basses with 24 frets access is improved because this cutaway is usually taken further into the bass.

The electrics on basses differ greatly from bass to bass. One of the commonest arrangements is with 3 controls and two pickups. Usually the first rotary control is master volume. The second is tone - on passive (non powered) basses tone controls are simply filters. Full off and the filter is doing nothing, full on and the maximum number of higher frequencies are filtered out, giveing the impression of bassy tone.

The neck pickup. This pickup is sometimes of the split pickup or "P" bass design. Whatever the design of this pickup, it will always give you bassier, richer sounds.

The Bridge; comprises four individual 'saddles' onto which each string rests. Ideally made of brass (for its qualities of sustain).

The saddles of the bridge are adjustable forward and backward and for height.

The height of each string is known as the action. A bass should never be set too low as you need to play quite hard and buzzing of the strings on frets is not usually desirable.

The bridge pickup; will give harder, more nasal sounds. This can be used on its own for tight funky fingerstyle sounds, but is more commonly mixed with the other pick-up.

Active basses are so called because the electrics are powered, usually by battery. This enables the design to be taken to extremes. Do take care if buying an active bass that the circuit is not noisy. There is no point having a wide range of sounds if the hiss created by the circuit is unbearable. A typical arrangement, such as found on the Status 2000 is to have a master volume control, a pick-up mix control and a bass cut and boost control and a treble cut and boost control. This provides a very wide range of sounds that are easy to find.

Some manufacturers have very powerful circuits, but these usually take a lot of setting up and learning.

The slow stretch exercise - the most important exercise for the left hand as it develops the muscle structure required to keep the hand and fingers in the correct position.

When studying the following exercises, ensure that you constantly refer to the photographs on pages 3 & 4.

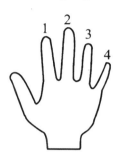

Left hand fingering. The diagram shows the left hand, with the palm facing you.

This exercise is designed to develop the muscle structure of the left hand. Start by positioning your hand so that the 1st finger is positioned right behind the 5th fret. (This is known as 5th position.) Then position 2nd behind the 6th fret, 3rd behind 7th fret 4th behind the 8th fret. The exercise begins with all the fingers held down on the 'G' string. If you find it hard at first to form the correct shape on the 'G' string then begin on the 'A' string and once the shape is formed slowly transfer to the G string. Play each note 4 times, beginning with the note being played by the 4th finger. Next move the 1st finger onto the D string, 5th fret, and play 4 times. Make sure that all the other fingers stay in position on the G string. Next move the 2nd finger onto the 6th fret of the D string, play 4 times. (The 3rd and 4th fingers should still be in place on the G string.) Next move the 3rd finger onto the 7th fret of the D string, play 4 times (keep the 4th finger in position on the G) and finally move the 4th finger onto the 8th fret of the D string and play 4 times. Repeat this procedure for moving to the A string and then the E string. When you have all four fingers in position on the E string repeat the procedure from the E string to the A string. The fingers move in the same order, 1,2,3,4. Don't be surprised if it is much harder working in this direction. You may find it nearly impossible to move your 3rd finger across the fingerboard while still holding the 4th finger in position. Once again persevere, it doesn't matter if it is days or even weeks before you can do this exercise with the fingers staying in shape and the third finger being able to move on it's own. What does matter is that you keep trying to keep your fingers in shape. As you will know after first completing the exercise the strain of keeping your fingers in position for a few minutes is considerable. You may even be in complete agony. However, by ensuring that you practise this exercise once or twice every day you will very quickly become comfortable with holding the hand in this position. If you find 5th position too strenuous, try and play the exercise towards you by a couple of frets, in 7th position.

Example

TARGET TECHNIQUE

Right hand finger-style technique, alternate fingers - *Practising the development of your benchmark technique.*

Play slowly and steadily, alternating the index and middle fingers of the right hand. Squeeze the notes by building up pressure on the string before playing through the string. Listen to ensure that each note you play has attack and then dies away.

Play each string for at least 30 seconds. Watch your right hand the whole time. Visually check that the angle the fingers strike the string is consistent on each string individually and as you change strings. Maintaining the same striking angle will greatly help you achieve a consistent sound. The most important point to remember is that as you change strings the position of your hand relative to the bridge will change. When playing the G string, your hand will be about 4 inches from the bridge. By the time you have reached the E string you should be just over an inch from the bridge. The exact position is worked out by listening. The same tone should be heard on each string. If you were to keep the hand the same distance from the bridge for all strings the tone would change from string to string, almost like changing basses mid way through the exercise.

Continuous four finger fluency exercise - *An exercise designed to get all the fingers working smoothly, if slowly - your first taste of co-ordinating both hands.*

Start by placing all four fingers in 5th position on the G string (as if you were about to begin the slow stretch exercise). Release fingers 2,3 and 4, but try to 'hover' them about ¼ inch above the string. Don't worry if you can't keep them this close early on, but do try your best to 'hover' them no more than an inch away and in their correct fret areas.

Play one note on each following the finger pattern 1-2-3-4 on the G string, then repeat on the D, A and E strings. Then repeat the E string (keeping the same finger order 1-2-3-4) and then the A, D and G strings. You should arrive back where you started having played each string twice.
The next stage is to move your hand towards the body of the guitar by one position (so that your first finger is now behind the 6th fret - 6th position) and repeat the process. Then move to 7th position and repeat then 8th position etc. Try and set an initial target of starting in 5th position and, moving one position at a time, end up in 12th position.

As you improve you must ensure that the right hand is working correctly when playing this and any other exercise.

Example

Major scale

The major scale is your first exercise to introduce both a technical challenge and the sound of music. You need to pay special attention to the workings of both hands. Play slowly so that you can concentrate on, and control the accuracy of both hands. Try to make each note sound right up to the next note so that you get a smooth unbroken sound. If you can avoid gaps between notes then the scale will sound musical even if you are playing it very slowly.

Example

Pentatonic scale

This will probably become your most used scale. There must be more bass riffs out there that use the pentatonic scale than any other, especially in the rock, blues and soul fields.

Example

Please ensure that when studying all the topics in this section that you refer back to the chapter, "In the Beginning", where there are photographs showing the correct postion of the hands and arms as well as technical information.

TARGET 1 MUSICIANSHIP

	4th String	3rd String	2nd String	1st String
open	E	A	D	G
	F	A#/Bb	D#/Eb	G#/Ab
	F#/Gb	B	E	A
3rd ●	G	C	F	A#/Bb
	G#/Ab	C#/Db	F#/Gb	B
5th ●	A	D	G	C
	A#/Bb	D#/Eb	G#/Ab	C#/Db
7th ●	B	E	A	D
	C	F	A#/Bb	D#/Eb
9th ●	C#/Db	F#/Gb	B	E
	D	G	C	F
	D#/Eb	G#/Ab	C#/Db	F#/Gb
12th ●●	E	A	D	G

Register

| LOW |
| MID |
| HIGH |

Fingerboard; concept and learning process.

The musical alphabet comprises the first seven letters of the normal alphabet. It only uses seven letters because music typically only uses seven notes at any one time. When a letter is on it's own (A-B-C-D-E-F-G) it is called a "Natural Note". These natural notes are usually spaced two frets apart on the bass. This distance, or interval, is called a Tone. There are two exceptions to this 'rule'. The interval (distance) from E to F and from B to C is only 1 fret. This interval is called a semitone. Make sure you are confident in this aspect before you begin learning the fingerboard. When you understand which notes are a tone apart and which are a semitone apart, you can begin (simply using one finger to point at note positions) to locate each note on the string working from the open string towards the bass, one note at a time. Say the note names aloud as you point to each one. As you'll see from the fingerboard chart, you will always move alphabetically from any given starting position. For example on the 'A' string, start with open A, then the 2nd fret (one tone from the open string) will be B, then the 3rd fret (one semitone from B) will be C, the 5th fret D etc. until the string becomes un-playable. Repeat this process on all strings frequently until you find naming the natural notes in this way easy. You will notice that when you name natural notes by moving from the open string to the guitar end of the neck that at the 12th fret you 'start again' with the set of seven notes. The twelfth fret is the eighth note that you have named. This eighth note in a successive sequence of natural notes is known as an octave. An octave has the same note name as the note you started on, in this case its the same as the open string. An octave is also mathematically related to the starting note as it is exactly twice the frequency of that starting note (assuming that you have gone from open string to 12th fret).

You will by now have noticed that the total number of notes or frets from the open string to the octave is twelve. To allow for these 'additional notes' (the function of which will be explained later in "Keys and Scales"), the names sharp (#) and flat (b) can be applied to any natural note, e.g. Ab or A# etc.. The addition of sharp and flat names added to each of the first seven letters of the alphabet clearly gives more than 12 options and so there is a means of describing every note that may be required.

Note names are central to your ability to really know your instrument. You cannot communicate with other musicians effectively if you do not know where to find specific notes on the bass. It could easily be argued that knowing where to find notes on your fingerboard is the single most important aspect of musicianship.

The above fingerboard chart illustrates very graphically the problems that bass players (and guitar players) have in learning the fingerboard. Your first impressions that the fingerboard is a jumble of notes is totally correct. Unlike a piano keyboard which lays out all notes in the same pattern for each octave, the fingerboard of guitars and basses is a mess. The keyboard also illustrates immediately all the natural notes, these are all the white keys on the keyboard. In this respect, keyboard players have it easy. Bass players have to try and develop their knowledge of their fingerboard in such a way that they can see all the natural notes as easily as if they were all painted white.

Jaco Pastorius - Bass player with Weather Report. His 1st solo album released in the late 70's was a milestone. He brought the fretless bass to everyone's attention. He also showed what could be done with harmonics, creating a whole piece (Portrait of Tracy) around them.

Concentrate entirely on learning the natural notes at first. You can always easily find sharp notes if required by remembering that a sharp note is a semitone or a fret higher than the natural, the flat note is a semitone lower than the natural. (The words sharp and flat can be applied to all natural notes.)

[N.B. When I talk about a note being higher or lower than another, I am referring to the pitch (frequency) of the note. So for example, a semitone higher, means one fret towards you and of course, a semitone lower, means one fret away from you. This sometimes causes confusion as beginners often refer to the top of their instrument as the head-stock.]

Scales and keys, basic outline

Scales and keys are two commonly used words in music. The simplest definition of a scale is that it is a sequence of notes, usually this means a sequence of seven notes, which explains why music has adopted only the first 7 letters of the alphabet. This sequence is most commonly made up of a mixture of tones (2 fret intervals) and semitones (1 fret intervals). The major scale, for example, has the sequence; tone - tone - semitone - tone - tone - tone - semitone. The minor scale has the sequence tone - semitone - tone - tone - semitone - tone - tone. This variation in tones and semitones is enough to completely change the character of the scale. The character of the major scale is positive and bright, whereas the minor is more ponderous and melancholy. By composing music using one scale or another you can immediately affect the emotional direction of the music. The real importance of scales becomes apparent when you realise that often a whole piece of music can be built from the notes of a single scale. That is a mere seven notes. The word key is used to label a given set of seven notes. For example the notes C, D, E, F, G, A, B (all the natural notes) are referred to as the key of C major. Put the other way round, if one musician communicates to another that he/she is going to play in the key of C major, the other musician knows that the seven notes in question are all going to be natural notes, centring around C. It is important to realise that notes are not equal in a key. The key of C major is not just about seven natural notes but also about the note C being heard as the most important note. The note C will sound as though every other note is revolving around it. There is a complete hierarchy of notes, with C - the key note, being the most important. This hierarchy will be discussed in more detail as you progress through this book.

Stanley Clarke - Originally became known in the 70's playing with Chick Corea and Return To Forever. In the late 70's he released his 3rd solo album "School Days", this album was one of my biggest influences and has remained one of the bass players albums to have to this day.

Stuart Hamm - Showed the world how to be versatile and virtuoso with 2 hand tapping. Although by no means the only exponent of two hand tapping, he stands out from the crowd because of his compositional and arrangement skills. His tuition video is one of the better videos about this style of bass playing that you can buy. Plus listen to his solo album; "Radio Free Albemuth"

TARGET 1
PLAYING & READING

Throughout this book I will be using both conventional music notation and tablature. You should try and understand how to play music from the conventional music notation, using tab to check the correct fret position for each finger. Tab is not a good form of notation for reading at sight, so in the sight reading sections it is omitted. Overall be positive towards reading music, it is quite straightforward, and actually enables you to see the plan of the music at a glance.

Pitch Notation

Before pitch can be established on the staff, you need to assign a clef. A clef is really a global frequency sign, saying whether the music is for a bass or treble instrument. As bass players we would expect to see the Bass Clef. In addition to stating that the music is for a bass instrument (or voice) the bass clef, which is also the 'F' clef tells us where to find 'F'. It does this by 'highlighting' the second line from the top, notice the heavy dot in the centre of the sign and the two small dots either side of this line. Once a note is assigned in this manner, all other notes are automatically assigned. This works because each line and space that is created by the staff represents a different letter of the alphabet.

Example

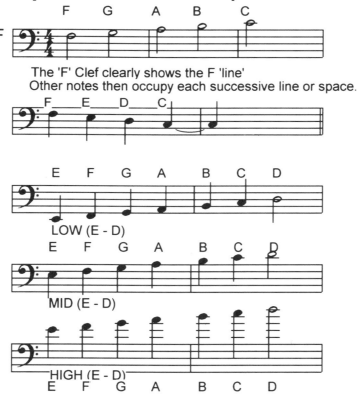

The 'F' Clef clearly shows the F 'line'
Other notes then occupy each successive line or space.

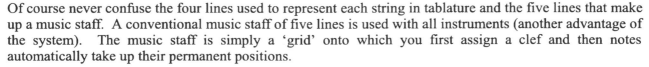

Of course never confuse the four lines used to represent each string in tablature and the five lines that make up a music staff. A conventional music staff of five lines is used with all instruments (another advantage of the system). The music staff is simply a 'grid' onto which you first assign a clef and then notes automatically take up their permanent positions.

One of the big advantages of reading music, as opposed to using tab, is that by glancing at a piece of music you can immediately see the rise and fall of the notes, the range of notes for a whole piece. In fact, with a bit of practise and experience you will soon be able to form a fairly accurate impression of how the music sounds by just glancing at the music page. This is not at all possible with tab. Of course the good thing about tab is that the precise fret location is laid out for you and it is primarily for this reason that it's included in this book.

Rhythm notation

Rhythm notation cannot be avoided, as its the same for tab and conventional notation. For now concentrate on the basic elements and the basic arithmetic of rhythm.

Example

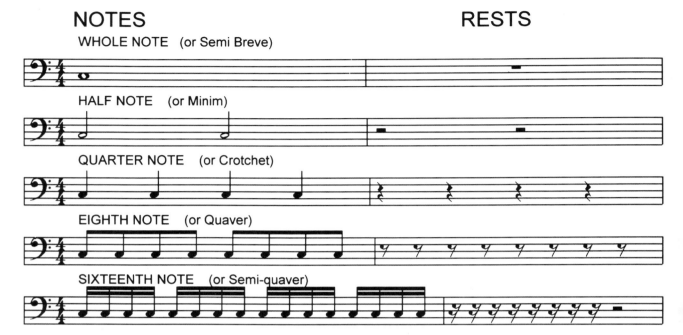

NOTES — RESTS

WHOLE NOTE (or Semi Breve)

HALF NOTE (or Minim)

QUARTER NOTE (or Crotchet)

EIGHTH NOTE (or Quaver)

SIXTEENTH NOTE (or Semi-quaver)

As you can see from the chart there are six main symbols used, each one represents half the length of the previous symbol. (There are more than six elements, however, you are unlikely to encounter anything higher than sixteenth notes until your playing is quite advanced.) Before trying to play any of these elements and trying to hear what they sound like, you need to appreciate that the elements represent relative values only. In other words the length of any element is dependent on first establishing a tempo. Tempo is the speed of the beat. A tempo can be set anywhere from 20 beats per minute to 300 beats per minute. For now think of a tempo of 60 beats per minute, use your watch to set this beat, 1 beat per second. This you'll soon realise is a very slow beat, but it will be fine for now. However, this still doesn't mean anything until we assign one of the six elements of rhythm to represent this beat. Most commonly, musicians assign a quarter note (crotchet) for this purpose. We can now describe each element as a precise time value, because, having set our tempo to 60 beats per minute and assigned the quarter note to the beat we can say that the quarter note will sustain for 1 second, the half note will sustain for 2 seconds and the whole note will sustain for 4 seconds. Eighth notes will of course sustain for ½ a second each.

To further clarify the chart, you begin with a whole note (also known as a semibreve, which is a clear oval shape with no (vertical) stem attached. This (for now) represents the longest note, in other words to play a whole note the sound is sustained for a count of four beats (4 seconds @ 60 B.P.M.). The half note (also known as a minim) is a clear oval with a stem and is sustained for a count of two beats (2 seconds @ 60 B.P.M.), The quarter note (also known as a crotchet) is a solid oval with a stem and sustains for one beat (1 second @ 60 B.P.M.), the eighth note (also known as a quaver) is a solid oval with both a stem and at the top of the stem either a beam, which is used to join to another eighth note, or a hook (flag) which can best be thought of as the beam folded down when the eighth note is on its own. The eighth note will sustain for ½ a beat (½ a second @ 60 B.P.M.). The sixteenth note (also known as a semiquaver) is a solid oval with both a stem and at the top of the stem either a double beam, or a double hook (flag). The sixteenth note will sustain for just ¼ of a beat (¼ second @ 60 B.P.M.).

A good way to get the hang of how each of these elements looks is to practise drawing them, copy out some music from the book and label each element that you come to, copy the rhythm notation chart perhaps.
An additional aspect of music and rhythm notation is the need to notate silence. Silence is a very important part of music as it creates vivid contrast to sound, this may seem very obvious, but it is important that as musicians we treat the length of silence with as much accuracy as the length of sound. For this reason each

element of sound has an equivalent element of silence. Elements of silence are called RESTS.

You should now be ready to begin listening to these element or sound lengths. Firstly, get your watch out again and count the seconds in groups of four. Grouping in four 1,2,3,4,1,2,3,4, etc. will naturally create a slight emphasis on the 1st beat. If you don't feel this then make a point of stressing the "1". 1,2,3,4,1,2,3,4,1 keep in time with each second of your watch so that you maintain the tempo at 60 B.P.M. Keeping the tempo, or speed of the beat constant, is a fundamental requirement in all music. As a bass player, you will always be a member of a bands rhythm section, and so time keeping, will need to be your area of expertise. In order to keep the tempo at 60, (or any other speed that you decide to set) you need to activate your 'internal body clock'. This is a mental discipline not an undiscovered organ in your body. However, it is good to imagine it being buried deep within your chest (a persons ability to keep time may well have something to do with the heart-beat - who knows). Whatever lies at the root of peoples' ability to keep time you have to first activate this ability and then work at developing it. Tapping your foot is one of the best ways of focusing your mind on the beat and speed and consistency of the beat. The foot creates a physical bond with the beat and ideally should influence the rest of the body to move with or feel the beat also.

An unfortunate consequence of concentrating is that we tend to stiffen up. As you develop your rhythmic abilities try continually to relax, keep the body feeling fluid, and continually try to feel the body moving in time with the beat.

The foot tap should concentrate on keeping the beat. It never taps out the rhythm of the music (unless you are playing ¼ notes) it must stay on the beat. So by now you should have your foot tapping once per second, maintaining a tempo of 60 B.M.P. Select any one note on the bass with the left hand and pluck with the right hand on the first beat of each bar. You should of course be counting the beats out loud, as well as tapping your foot. By repeating your playing on just the first beat of each bar (group of 4) and keeping the note sustaining you are playing whole notes. Now, in addition to playing on the 1st beat, play also on the 3rd beat. If the notes are sustaining one to the next, you will now be playing half notes. If this goes OK for a while, try playing on each beat. You will now be playing quarter notes, and your foot tap, counting out loud and bass notes should all be together.

Stop playing and take another look at your watch. Were you still playing at 60 B.P.M. or did you speed up during the exercise. Reset the tempo by counting 1,2,3,4,1,2,3,4, with you watch, introduce your foot tap to this count. You now have to learn to divide the beat into smaller increments of time. To start with we are only concerned with dividing the beat into two. This will enable you to play eighth notes both individually and in combination with other elements. Introduce a mid-way point to your counting out loud. Count "&" between each beat; 1 & 2 & 3 & 4 & 1 & 2 & 3 & 4 & etc. Make sure that you speak clearly and accurately when you do this. There should be a precise rhythm in the way you speak this count. The &'s should be right in the middle of the beat so that each count is ½ second. Getting back to the bass, try and play quarter notes along to this new count. Your playing should be with your foot tap and the main numbers (beats) only and you should still be able to clearly say "&" in the middle of each beat. If this goes OK and your foot is not put off by the new count, try and play with your full 1 & 2 & 3 & 4 &1 & 2 & 3 & 4 & count. You will now be playing continuous eighth notes. This may not be easy the first time you try it, but persevere, try and remain patient before moving on to other challenges rhythmically. One problem might be that as soon as you start trying to play eighth notes, everything is working properly apart from the foot, which has suddenly decided to do its own thing. Keep working at it until everything is under control and in its correct place.

James Jamerson - The great Motown bass player. Jamerson is arguably the best ever pop bass player. Essentially a true jazz musician, his skill, invention and phenomenal grooves not only supported hit after hit in the sixties for Motown records but he has inspired more bass players than anyone else. It is probably true to say that in the UK, whilst many of us were being influenced and inspired by him, no one knew his name. A recently released book "Standing In The Shadows Of Motown", the life and work of James Jamerson by Dr Licks, is an essential.

The following riffs are designed to bring together basic technique and simple rhythms.

Example

Learning Basslines in this book

Whether you're learning a two bar riff or a piece several pages long, the approach for practice will be more or less the same.

1. Break the music down phrase by phrase. (A musical phrase is not necessarily one bar, however, most bass lines are like musical commands and so very often 1 bar does represent a complete phrase or suitable component of a phrase that can be broken down.)

2. Learn the rhythm of the bar or phrase.

3. Research where to find each note, and determine which finger will play which note. (Throughout this book you can use the tab to find out which string and fret to play a note, and usually I have indicated the best finger to use.)

4. Practise the pattern of notes first, without attempting to add the rhythm.

5. Put the notes and rhythm together.

6. Repeat for the next bar or phrase.

7. Join phrases (bars) one and two together.

8. Continue by adding a phrase (bar) at a time, joining on to the previously learned sections as you go. On a very long piece, you would break the music down into its main sections (verse, chorus etc.) and learn each section separately.

9. When the whole piece, or section is learned roughly, you need to make a decision as to what aspect of the piece you will practise:

a) Either to play the piece (or section) from start to finish with the emphasis placed on not hesitating or losing time. When you attempt a piece from start to finish, you must not stop - don't worry about mistakes, not even big mistakes, the priority is to keep going and to not make any mistakes in timing. Taken to extremes, if the first note is in time and the last note is in time then your priorities have been correct for this method of practice. Practising in this way ensures that you learn that time is your number 1 priority. You can never get away with timing errors, or losing your place in performance of any kind. The occasional note played wrong may not even be noticed in a recording session. When gigging, a few wrong notes will be noticed by no-one but yourself.

b) If when trying to play from start to finish, you make serious errors in the same place time after time, then you clearly need to re-examine the point in the music where these errors occur. Learn to pick up the music a few notes before the error section and stop at the end of the error section. If necessary start again, looking again at the rhythm. Are you able to count it out loud if you want to. If the answer to this is no, or the occasional number is not spoken clearly, then this indicates that you do not understand the rhythm, or are not in control of the rhythm. Really slow the section down until everything is consciously controlled. Make sure the foot-tap is under control as well. Look at the fingering, play very slowly and try and make sure the fingers are always moving in anticipation of future events. The further ahead you can think, the less likely you are to get stuck. Are you playing the notes in the best possible locations.

Most error sections are self-inflicted by rushing the original learning sessions. Patience when first learning, playing more slowly at first, will reduce the need to constantly re-examine music that you learn.

Once you've dealt with these riffs make sure that you have read and studied Ear Training - Target 1 and then try the following riffs.

When you have learned how to basically play all of these short basslines, so that you know where to find the notes and you can control the rhythm you need to re-think your entire approach.

Up to now you have had to study the basics of rhythm and note identification. You have had to get over the basics of technique and you have had to concentrate hard just to reach this point. You now need to start thinking how to *really* play these lines.

A great many basslines, even on hit records, and even on some highly regarded pieces of music, are technically very simple. Often they are rhythmically quite simple too. However, what is going to count is how you play the lines. The sound of every note. The consistency of your time-keeping. Your ability to groove and therefore communicate emotional ideas to the listener is what its all about. You may think that you have enough to think about at this stage but I believe that the sooner you acknowledge these essentials about bass playing the better.

In the Playing & Reading sections of this book I will be drawing your attention to points of Feel and Groove all the time. The secret to having a groove is basically the ability to work hard enough to achieve real consistency in every aspect of your playing but especially **TIMING AND SOUND.**

Bassline 1.

Constant eighth notes appear at first to be one of the simpler rhythmic patterns in bass playing. Unfortunately simple, straight ahead rhythms demand absolute perfection to work. Anyone listening is able to scrutinise these patterns and will hear and feel the slightest imperfections. As this may be the first bassline you ever learn perfection is not expected. However, you need to start now to work towards this goal. Eighth notes are usually kept in very strict time, so if you have a drum machine, set the hi-hat to constant eighth notes and try to ensure that your playing is tight with this hi-hat. Make sure that your foot is tapping without wavering from the main (quarter note) beat. Counting 1 & 2 & 3 & 4 & is probably necessary at first. If you don't need to count out loud to understand the rhythm then you still need to 'feel' this subdivision. Some players use subtle body movement to maintain this feel for the subdivision, a kind of dance, some 'speak' a percussive count. It is best when starting to count out loud and over time allow this count to be replaced by a less spoken number orientated counting method. (If you stop counting numbers (consciously) make sure that you don't lose awareness of which beat you are playing.)

It is not enough to merely play each note in perfect time. You also have to ensure that each note is played with the same weight and that each note is plucked using the same finger angle, so that the tone is matched. A good starting point with Bassline 1 is to try and get every note evenly matched and level all the way through. This is not easy, but try and keep trying.

When you can achieve reasonable consistency you then need to introduce some accents. Accents are naturally present forces in music. In Ear Training - Target 1, you are encouraged to speak the "1" louder than the other beats. This to some extent will happen naturally and is why music tends to group into fours or threes etc. In 4/4 time, the first of each group of four beats contains the accent. With bassline 1, try and play the first note of each bar slightly louder than all the other notes to create this accent. Exaggerate at first to get the feel, physically, of how to achieve this. Once your right hand is used to the idea, relax more until the accent is quite subtle. This will make the bassline much more musical and very much more exiting. Accenting correctly and consistently is a major part of the art of bass playing.

Bassline 2.

Bassline 2 is quite easy, but this does not mean that it couldn't be a real bass line generating real power. Try and imagine this one in a big rock venue setting, imagine also that it is perhaps solo bass or with a simple thudding drum beat behind it. You have to create and deliver this power. Tonal consistency is your real battle with this riff. All the dotted half notes have to be struck exactly in the right place with equal  force. It is vital with this riff that each note has a positive attack. The tone needs to be hard, but full of bass. Try playing about 1½ inches from the bridge on the bass string, keep the end joint of the striking finger (I'd use middle finger) firm. Of course the timing must be spot on. Make sure these long notes sustain fully, there should be no gap between the long held notes and the notes played on beat 4. The shorter notes on beat 4 can be cut slightly short (articulated), this will help accentuate the main long notes. Each long note should match for volume (level) and tone and each short note should match for tone and level.

Bassline 3.

This bassline implies a stress that isn't on the beat. When a note is played on the offbeat, and is tied to the note on the beat (i.e. sustains across the beat) the effect is to anticipate that beat. This almost always means that you treat the anticipation as if it were on the beat. So in this bassline the first note is accented and the note on the off-beat of the second beat is accented (2 &). (If you're programming a drum machine for this riff, place the kick drum on beat 1 and on 2 &, snare on the second and fourth beats and have a continuous eighth note hi-hat. A real drum part would be a bit more involved but this will give you the basics.) The trick to this line is to keep it rock steady with each accented note matched for tone and level, and all unaccented notes matched for tone and level.

Bassline 4.

Very similar in feel to Bassline 3. The anticipation is on every other bar. Anticipating the first beat this time.

Bassline 5.

On the surface quite an easy riff, provided you have understood the dotted quarter note, eighth note rhythm. However, making it sound light and easy going is actually a little more tricky than it seems. The main difficulty lies in the fact that you have to play every note on a different string. This makes tone matching very difficult. Also you have really three different weights to apply to the various notes, depending on their position in the bar. Beat one is the main group accent and will therefore be slightly harder and louder than the other notes. (Remember that each first beat should match the other first beats.) The notes on the off beats (2 & and 4 &) should be quite light, but should all match each other. The third beat is not quite so important as the first so should be firm but slightly less than the first beat. (Again every note on the third beat should match for level and tone.)

Remember these different weights should be quite subtle, the over-riding effect should be that the whole riff sounds very even with perfect tone match from string to string. Your right hand will have to move quite a bit to accommodate this latter point. Probably notes on the E string will be played about 1 inch from the bridge, notes played on the A string about 2 inches from the bridge and notes on the D string about 2½ inches from the bridge. The open strings in the final bar move a little further from the bridge, about 1½ inches and play with the finger a little flatter than normal.

Bassline 6.

Because of the rhythm used in the opening bar and because the rhythmic concept is to incorporate a lot of notes played off the beat, you wouldn't interpret any of the off beat notes as anticipating the following beat and therefore would not accent them. Typically, a lighter touch is achieved on the off-beats by articulating the notes slightly shorter than written. The main difficulty in this riff is keeping it musical and even sounding.

Bassline 7.

The safest interpretation of a bassline that is made up of almost equal parts of sound and silence (rests) is to play all the notes for their maximum written length and ensure that the rests are executed cleanly and that the silence begins exactly on time. In order to time your rests very accurately and to ensure that there are no unwanted noises produced by stopping a note, create the rest with a right hand finger first, then take the pressure off the left hand to make sure that there is absolutely no ring.

Try playing this bassline quite aggressively, making almost every note seem like a power note. Of course, the first beat should always have that little bit more.

Basline 8.

A two bar riff, and very much a two bar rhythmic concept. Don't rush the learning of this one. When the second bar differs considerably from the first rhythmically, control of the whole can take time to acquire.

The idea is a reggae impression. Reggae typically uses the bass as a sound you feel rather than hear. To achieve this the electrics need to be set to maximum neck pickup and the bass control turned up high on active basses or maximum filter of higher frequencies on passive basses (You will probably think of this as off, or no tone added). Also in reggae the weight of accent on beats one and three is both equal and more exaggerated than with most other styles. Make sure the accents are heavier (bassier), rather than louder.

I hope the above guidelines for playing what seemed like nice easy riffs to get you started have not left you scratching your head and wondering whether it's worth continuing playing bass. Welcome to the world of real bass playing. You may think that you are not ready for such detail yet. I believe that the sooner you start trying to make the bass groove the better. Groove is achieved primarily by playing with total consistency in both timing and sound. The ability to deliver a great groove will ensure you play with the best bands and work most often.

Main performance points:

Timing errors are unacceptable. Put a lot of effort into maintaining the flow of a piece of music. Note errors are not usually noticed (within reason) so ignore them while playing from start to finish. Decide where the accented notes are and keep them consistent. Make sure all notes are tone matched. Play often with either a metronome or drum machine and try and get tighter and tighter with this 'perfect' time.

Example

Using the A pentatonic scale to create simple riffs.

In your study of technique, you will during your first target period learn how to play the A pentatonic scale. Although you still have much to learn from the other topics in Target 1 before serious composition or improvisation can be started, you can use this scale to begin experimenting with composition.

One point to bear in mind about composing (and improvising) is that you need to practise it and always be doing some form of composition.

Try at first to play through the scale. Now look at which notes you are playing and try and memorise them, as it is going to be very helpful to remember each note name, which finger plays it and where. Your first task is to try and invent a simple one bar riff. The pentatonic scale has five different notes, plus you know where the octave of A is as well. Keep to just these six notes for now. Start by selecting just 3 notes. You could do this at random, or if you prefer play low A and then try each note of the scale after A to see which note sounds best for your second note. Then when you have selected your second note experiment to find you favourite third note. You now have the three notes selected for your first riff. Adding a rhythm to these notes will give you your riff. When you have just started playing bass getting any rhythm can seem impossible. Start by trying what you know. Quarter notes, eighth notes, mixtures of quarter and eighth notes. (Obviously, if you only have three notes in your riff and your rhythm has, perhaps, 8 eighth notes some or all of your notes need to be repeated). If your composition so far doesn't seem too interesting then try 'borrowing' a rhythm from a record. Choose a rhythm that you can easily imitate, although don't worry too much if you don't understand what exactly makes it up, and certainly don't worry if you haven't a clue as to how it might be written down.

Example

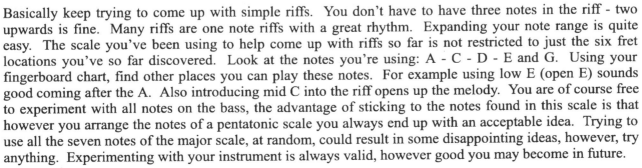

Basically keep trying to come up with simple riffs. You don't have to have three notes in the riff - two upwards is fine. Many riffs are one note riffs with a great rhythm. Expanding your note range is quite easy. The scale you've been using to help come up with riffs so far is not restricted to just the six fret locations you've so far discovered. Look at the notes you're using: A - C - D - E and G. Using your fingerboard chart, find other places you can play these notes. For example using low E (open E) sounds good coming after the A. Also introducing mid C into the riff opens up the melody. You are of course free to experiment with all notes on the bass, the advantage of sticking to the notes found in this scale is that however you arrange the notes of a pentatonic scale you always end up with an acceptable idea. Trying to use all the seven notes of the major scale, at random, could result in some disappointing ideas, however, try anything. Experimenting with your instrument is always valid, however good you may become in future.

Hearing the Bass:

It may sound odd at first to ask, can you hear the notes you are playing on the bass. Of course you can hear them as musical sound but the question is, can you truly distinguish the pitch of the notes? The (simple) test for this is to play a note on the bass (any note will do, although it is sensible to play a common note such as a note found in 2nd position) listen carefully to the note, now sing the note (Yes, sing - a lot of you reading this will break out in a sweat at the thought of having to sing but using your voice to confirm that you are hearing sound correctly is going to be essential to developing your ear). When you sing the note, listen again and try again. A lot of students will pass this test easily in which case try a few more notes at random and then move onto the next section. For those that aren't sure if the notes being sung are the same as the notes being played on the bass - don't worry, it's not uncommon for this to be a problem at first. Your only answer to the problem is to keep trying. Listen again to the note, try and hear the sound form in your mind before you attempt to use your voice to pitch the note. If it's still difficult, or difficult to be sure, try playing a higher note as you may find that the pitch of higher notes is easier to determine. If after several attempts you still feel that things are not right, leave it and move on. You may need to get a bit more used to using your voice, as it is possible that you cannot yet pitch with your voice what you hear. However, it is more likely that you are not yet hearing correctly and only hear an impression of the sound, not its true pitch.

The major scale - singing slowly.

Your first exercise is to practise singing the major scale. This is partly to get the voice used to what is very possibly a new and reluctant role but mainly the exercise is helping you understand the very foundation of musical sound - the major scale. As all music has a close relationship with this scale understanding it and the distance between each of the notes is very important.

Your first step is to find the lowest note that you can comfortably sing. Try and find out what note this is so that you can write it down and remember your 'voice key'. Even those who have never sung a note before will quickly be able to sing all the notes of the scale. You may find that the octave seems very high at first, but it will soon come with practise.

[If there is one aspect of musicianship that I would like to convince you of with this book, it would be the importance and usefulness of using your voice to develop your hearing. Please keep trying if you find these early steps difficult or if you feel uncomfortable, you will gain great reward in the long term for work put in now.]

Once you have sung the scale a few times ascending, try and reverse the scale and descend. This is usually a little more difficult but won't take long to deal with. If you really find it difficult at first then play the scale on the bass as you sing. When you have sufficient confidence try and gradually phase this practice out.

For those that found the initial exercise of pitching notes played on the bass difficult or impossible, now is the time to return to playing notes, at random, on the bass to see if you are pitching them, and therefore hearing them more clearly. In 90% of cases, students who initially could not pitch notes on the bass in the beginning, can do so after they have learned to sing the major scale. In a few cases it may take a bit longer, although you don't want to attempt exercises beyond this point until you are positive that your major scale is being sung reasonably accurately and that you accurately pitch at least 90% of notes played on the bass at random.

Sing Slowly; you are trying to develop your hearing rather than your voice. Apart from making an effort to sustain each note by carefully controlling the exhalation of air as you sing and of course ensuring that the pitch remains the same for as long as you hold the note, this book will make no further effort to improve you as a singer. However, if you do want to improve your voice either for lead or backing vocals, then all of the exercises in this section will greatly assist you in this goal.

When you have really got used to singing the scale slowly and are sure that the notes are accurate try a further enhancement; pause between each note. As you pause, really try to imagine the sound of the next note in your mind. When you think you have a sound, or an image of the sound in your mind, pitch (sing) the note. It is likely that if you are really *hearing* the sound before singing it, you will sing the note cleanly (no swooping up or down until you finally get the note right).

Rhythm; the importance of the basic elements. Rhythm needs to be considered as ear training because, as with pitch recognition, it is important to recognise instinctively rhythm and rhythm patterns. It is not enough for most situations to be able to work out a rhythm that another musician is using, or that you hear on a record, taking many minutes or even hours to work it out. You need to be able to immediately recognise and understand as much rhythm as possible.

The basic elements of rhythm are the whole note, the half note, the quarter note and the eighth note. Without complete understanding of these simple elements you are unlikely to develop your rhythm abilities. The more surprising aspect is really that as you get better, these basics remain just as important. For the more advanced player, the basic elements of rhythm are used to really practice and understand the incredible accuracy that is required of top bass players. Realising this now will hopefully ensure that you try to play cleanly and accurately from the beginning. This is as much an attitude as a technical skill.

Metronomes and Drum Machines.

All bass players need to own either a metronome or a drum machine. A metronome is the cheapest option, but it will only give a click on the beat, whereas a drum machine can be programmed to give anything from a metronome beat to all the drum patterns for a song. With the price of drum machines falling all the time, and especially with the price of second-hand drum machines being fairly low, I would always recommend that students of bass guitar buy a drum machine. Do not get old fashioned rhythm boxes, you need to be able to programme the machines and you need machines with a good clean bass drum, snare drum and hi-hat sound. (All other sounds are unimportant for your rhythm development, although they may be important for your song demos etc.). If you really can't afford either device at first, then don't worry. It is possible to make a good start with rhythm without them provided you are prepared to take real care and concentrate.

Both notation of these elements and basic time-keeping techniques are discussed in the Target 1, Reading & Playing section, so you must read this before moving onto the following exercises.

The next exercise is designed to familiarise you with hearing syncopation. This is where the notes are moved off the main beat to the off beat or &. The following exercise is a simple and common rhythm, however it is essential that you can play it without your foot beat being drawn to the off-beat. Your counting and foot-tap must be present strongly the whole time.

Example

1 & 2 & 3 & 4 &   1 & 2 & 3 & 4 &   1 & 2 & 3 & 4 &   1 & 2 & 3 & 4 &

> ***Marcus Miller** - For me, Marcus is THE complete bass player. He seems to excel in every department of bass playing. Great technique, in seemingly any style. A supreme composer and arranger his credits would take a book to list. Luther Vandross and legendary jazz trumpet player, Miles Davis. Can also be heard on most of alto sax man, David Sanborn's albums. He also has a number of solo albums - all are worth listening to. When you read in this book about timing and sound, listen to Marcus play and you'll understand exactly what I'm saying.*

Minor scale

Example

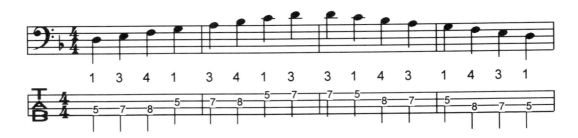

3rd finger exercise - *The third finger exercise is designed to increase finger independence. The 2nd and 3rd fingers are always going to be 'joined' to one another to some extent. However, in time the flexibility and independence can be increased.*

From a technical point of view, complete independence is highly desirable. This exercise is best done slowly, with the emphasis on trying to gently stretch the tendons rather than trying to see how fast you can go. So lift the third finger as high as possible, and press extra hard when you return the finger to the fretboard. Start by positioning the left hand in 5th position (1st finger behind the 5th fret) with the 1st and 2nd fingers on the D string, and the 3rd and 4th fingers on the A string. Keeping the 1st, 2nd and 4th fingers firmly on the fingerboard at all times move only the third finger back and fourth from the A string to the D string. The exercise should actually comprise 4 notes as follows . Even though the 3rd finger will not be responsible for sounding the F in this exercise always move it back to the 7th fret of the A string whenever you are sounding the F (which of course will be played by the 4th finger).

Don't be alarmed if you find this exercise nearly impossible or very painful at first, just do a little at a time and gradually increase both the length of time you spend doing the exercise and the height that you lift the 3rd finger.

Example

4-3-2-1 Stamina Exercise

Before you embark on this exercise you need to think about the technical process of finger release. Unlike putting fingers onto the fingerboard to make a note sound, which is quite a natural action, releasing fingers causes the hand all sorts of problems. The main problem is that as you release, for example - the 4th finger, the mechanism used to release the finger relaxes the muscles in the entire hand so that the finger shoots away from the bass, perhaps to its full extent, or 3 or 4 inches. This is enough to unbalance the entire hand causing it to lose its shape and make efficient playing impossible. So the real point of this exercise is to try and get some control over the finger release process. Therefore practise this exercise very slowly at first. Begin by placing all the fingers on the fingerboard. Slowly release the 4th finger, try and make sure it doesn't shoot out more than and inch or so, then release the 3rd taking care that this doesn't send both the 3rd and 4th fingers inches from the fingerboard, then release the 2nd finger. As you play the 1st finger try and get the 4th finger into position over the 8th fret of the D string. If you've controlled the hand then you won't have far to go, if you haven't controlled the hand then you may have to move the 4th finger 5 or 6 inches to reach this note. The distance fingers have to travel to reach notes will of course have a great influence on your playing ability. Players with good left hand technique will usually only move their fingers ½ an inch at most. This means that the left hand will not create unwanted noise, it will be quick and it will be easy. Good players always make even difficult lines look easy. This control of the fingers is one reason why it looks easy. The hard truth here is that it will take time to gain control over your fingers. The 4321 exercise is a vital exercise in developing your technique. Later in this book the same exercise and process of finger release will be explored in greater detail.

Example

Blues scale

The blues scale is really just an embellishment of the pentatonic scale. I always include the leading tone when playing the blues scale ascending. This is because whenever anybody plays in this scale the leading tone is nearly always used when ascending to the tonic (key note).

Example

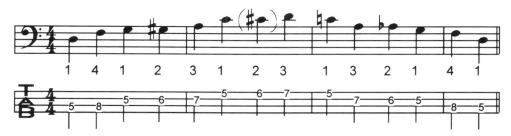

Fingerstyle treatment of octaves

Octaves are a great discovery for the beginner to bass guitar. The use of octaves in playing bass is considerable. They create an incredible amount of movement in the sound and therefore energy. Early in your playing career you can introduce octaves to increase energy and give your basslines considerable invention without having to know any more about composing basslines.

Firstly, left hand technique with octaves. Usually the fingers that play octaves will be 1st and 4th. Use of the 4th finger may to some seem like sloppy technique. This is not so. For one thing playing in as relaxed a manner as possible is a good idea, changing the muscles around (as opposed to keeping the hand in the same spot exactly for ½ an hour) is good technique. Also, think about all the scales you've so far learned. You would never play the note one fret above the octave (it's out of key) so there's no point in having your 4th finger wandering about with nothing to do. So an alternative to 1st and 4th would be 2nd and 4th. However, I'm sure that if you try this you'll quickly decide that 1st and 4th is much more comfortable. Also the next most common note to add to a bass line that contains octaves is the 5th note of the scale. This would be played by the 3rd finger, if 1st and 4th take care of root (original note) and octave.

The following exercises are designed to get the left hand used to a variety of possible scenarios for octave playing. When playing a lot of octaves the range of notes (from lowest to highest) is likely to be much greater than a part that is not using octaves. A span of two and a half octaves is not unusual in basslines employing a lot of octaves. This requires a very different approach to left hand technique.

Right hand technique. With octaves a slight variation to the 'rule' of alternating the middle and index fingers of the right hand is often useful. Generally with octaves, the idea is to play the lower note with the middle finger and the octave above with the index finger.

Example

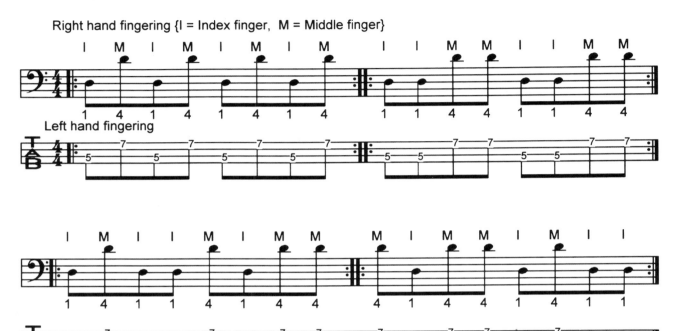

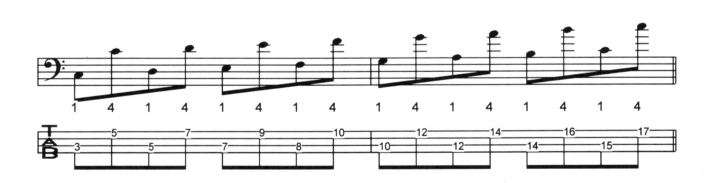

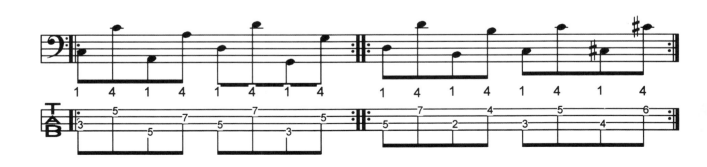

Dynamics And Tone Exercises For The Right Hand

If you are to really deliver basslines you need to develop your sound. The bass sound comes partly from the make and type of bass you have, the electronic settings on the bass, the amplifier and its settings but MAINLY from the way the strings are struck by the right hand fingers.

Dynamics: You need to develop a dynamic range in your playing, an ability to play from the softest 'whisper' right through to a fret buzzing blast of sound. Apply the following exercise to every string and practise each string for about 1 minute at least. Start playing, at normal volume, steady eighth notes at a very comfortable tempo. Gradually increase the force of playing (and therefore the volume) until you are 'over-playing'. This over-playing is usually characterised by fret buzz, although this does depend on how the bass is set up. From your hardest playing, gradually ease off, maintaining the tempo precisely and work towards the softest notes you can get. Keeping the tempo constant will enable you to assess your control. If the tempo wavers as you change the force of your playing then you are losing control. Go from normal playing to ultra hard, to ultra soft and back to normal. If this is done gradually it should take at least a minute to complete.

Tone or Timbre: The bass guitar produces a very rich sound. That is a sound full of frequencies or harmonics all at different volumes or levels. You always hear the main note, or fundamental frequency as the prime note, but all the component frequencies are contributing to the overall tone. By striking the strings in different ways, and with varying degrees of force a huge variety of sounds can be obtained. These sounds will enable you to communicate more emotions and messages to your audience. The first step is to learn how to achieve these sounds and have an exercise for exploring the possibilities. There are two principal ways to vary the tone on a bass.

1. Finger angle
2. Striking position (distance from the bridge)

1. To practice finger angle sounds, take one finger at a time and starting in your normal position, play regular steady notes, taking care to keep the force the same and bring your wrist back towards the body of the bass so that you strike the string gradually flatter and flatter until you are playing almost down on the string. Move back towards your normal position and then beyond, gradually curving the finger until it is plucking upwards into the palm of the hand. Gradually work your way back to the normal, base position.

2. To practice striking position, again work with one finger at a time. Begin in your normal starting position and keeping the angle and force constant, move the finger towards the bridge. As with all these exercises keep the speed of playing constant. Listen to the tone become harder as you move towards the bridge. When you are right up to the bridge (a position you would only use in exceptional circumstances) move towards the neck, slowly, observing the tone changes as you move. When you reach the neck gradually work back to the starting position.

N.B. With all right hand dynamic and tone exercises always start and finish in the positions you should still be working at as your base positions. It is very important that you have a line and force of playing that you regard as 'normal'. This way tone and volume changes can always be measured from this 'normal' position.

FENDER. *The most famous name in guitars and basses.*
Leo Fender invented the Bass Guitar. *The two best known*
basses are the Precision and the Jazz. *The Precision is*
identified by the fatter neck and single split pickup, whereas
the Jazz has a much slimmer, more tapered neck and a
separate neck and bridge pickup, for greater tonal variation.

Key signatures

So far you understand that a key describes a set of seven notes. However, the only key you so far know about is C major - seven natural notes with C as the key note. All other keys will contain combinations of either natural notes and sharp notes, or natural notes and flat notes. You never have mixtures of flat notes and sharp notes. For this reason keys are often thought of as either being 'sharp' keys or 'flat' keys. This has nothing to do with their sound, only that some contain sharp notes and some contain flat notes.

The reason this happens is the key system follows a simple logic; that each note of the scale be given a different letter of the alphabet for identification purposes. Therefore, whichever note begins a major scale each successive note will be the next letter of the alphabet which will ensure that sharps and flats are not mixed. For example, play a major scale beginning on F. By following the finger pattern you've learned in your Technique - target 1 study, and using the fingerboard chart to check your note names, you will find that the first note (played with the 2nd finger, of course) is F. The second note is G, the third A, and the fourth note will be called Bb. Notice that it cannot be called A# as you have just played a note called A. (There can be no repeated letters of the alphabet). After Bb you come on to C, then D and finally E. The last or 8th note of a scale is the octave, which is, from a key point of view, a repeat of the first note.

The number of sharps or flats a key has is used as a kind of code to communicate the key from musician to musician. A musician can indicate the key of a piece of music by informing musicians of either the number of sharp or flats (e.g. "this song's in 4 sharps", or pointing 4 fingers upwards (flats would be pointing down)), or more commonly the musician will say that the song or music is in the Key of E major. Whatever the method, the expectation is that you know and understand these codes. Remember that most pieces of music you're likely to find yourself playing are constructed around one principal key, or just seven notes. To start with you need to learn these codes. This will not immediately give you the facility to play fluently in any key, there is more to playing in a key than simply knowing the code, or how many sharps and flats there are in a key. (Note that by knowing how many sharps or flats there are in a key, and being able to identify what these sharp or flat notes are, you are easily able to work out which notes remain natural. Remember, the point of learning the codes - Key signatures - is to know immediately what all seven notes of the key are.)

The learning process: MAJOR KEYS

Firstly, concentrate on the sharp keys. By learning the following sequence of letters you will be able to calculate how many sharps there are in each of these keys: G, D, A, E, B, F#. There is one sharp note in G major, 2 sharp notes in D major, 3 sharps in A major and so on. Just keep repeating this sequence until it is memorised.

The next step is to be able to identify what notes are actually sharp. For this there is another sequence to learn: F, C, G, D, A, E, B. This is not going to be a difficult sequence to remember if you consider that it's the same as the first sequence with F and C added at the start. This sequence represents the sharp notes themselves.

The way to put both sequences together is as follows:
G major has one sharp (1st letter in top sequence), this sharp note is F sharp (the first letter of the 2nd sequence).
D major has two sharps (2nd in top sequence), these sharps are F sharp and C sharp (the first two letters in the 2nd sequence)
A major has three sharps (3rd letter in top sequence), these sharps are F sharp, C sharp and G sharp (the

first three letters in the 2nd sequence).
If you understand the above the following diagram should enable you to see how all the keys work.

Just in case you're still not sure the following should clarify each key:

C major = ALL NATURAL NOTES

LEARN THESE SEQUENCES to memorise other key signatures:

SHARP KEYS: **G -D - A - E - B - F# - C#**
ACTUAL SHARPS: **F# - C# - G# - D# - A# - E# - B#**

FLAT KEYS: **F - Bb - Eb - Ab - Db - Gb - Cb**
ACTUAL FLATS: **Bb - Eb - Ab - Db - Gb - Cb - Fb**

C MAJORKey signature = All natural notesC, D, E, F, G, A, B, (C).

SHARP KEYS

G MAJORKey signature = 1 sharp (F#)
G, A, B, C, D, E, F#, (G).
D MAJORKey signature = 2 sharps (F#,C#)D, E, F#, G, A, B, C# (D).
A MAJORKey signature = 3 sharps (F#,C#,G#)
A, B, C#; D, E, F#, G#, (A).
E MAJORKey signature = 4 sharps (F#,C#,G#,D#)
E, F#, G#, A, B, C#, D# (E).
B MAJORKey signature = 5 sharps (F#,C#,G#,D#,A#)
B, C#, D#, E, F#, G#, A#, (B).
F# MAJORKey signature = 6 sharps (F#,C#,G#,D#,A#, E#)
F#, G#, A#, B, C#, D#, E#, (F#)
C# MAJORKey signature = 7 sharps (F#,C#,G#,D#,A#, E#, B# - all sharp)
C#, D#, E#, F#, G#, A#, B#, (C#)

FLAT KEYS

F MAJORKey signature = 1 flat (Bb)
F, G, A, Bb, C, D, E, (F)
Bb MAJORKey signature = 2 flats (Bb, Eb)
Bb, C, D, Eb, F, G, A, (Bb).
Eb MAJORKey signature = 3 flats (Bb,Eb,Ab)
Eb, F, G, Ab, Bb, C, D, (Eb)
Ab MAJORKey signature = 4 flats (Bb,Eb,Ab,Db)
Ab, Bb, C, Db, Eb, F, G, (Ab)
Db MAJORKey signature = 5 flats (Bb,Eb,Ab,Db,Gb)
Db, Eb, F, Gb, Ab, Bb, C, (Db)
Gb MAJORKey signature = 6 flats (Bb,Eb,Ab,Db,Gb,Cb)
Gb, Ab, Bb, Cb, Db, Eb, F, (Gb)
Cb MAJORKey signature = 7 flats (Bb,Eb,Ab Db,Gb,Cb,Fb - all flats)

to see how keys signatures are described in written music refer to Playing & Reading - Target 2
3 chord trick and triads

You should understand now that in each key there are seven notes. These notes, of course, make up all of the melodic elements in a song but they also make up the notes of all the chords. A chord is defined as three or more notes sounding together - that is, heard harmonically. When notes are played at the same time, we don't easily hear the individual notes that make up that chord, we hear a single, rich sound. This is known as harmony. So a harmonic progression is a chord progression. The knowledge of chords is of major importance, especially to the improvising musician. Chords need to be known by sound and by understanding the individual notes that make them up.

As a bass player, your need to understand chords is about as great as those instrumentalists, such as keyboard players and guitarists, who are actually playing chords all the time. Even though as bass players we rarely play chords it is vital to understand chords. Without chord knowledge we cannot understand the composition, we will not be able to determine the key of the music, and we will certainly never be able to improvise very well.

For the moment, consider that all songs and pieces of music are based on a harmonic, or chord progression. Typically, in practice, the only information we get about a song is the chord progression. From this we have to be able to compose a bass line. In order to compose a good bass line, we need to be able to get as much information about the song from just the chords as we can. Fortunately, chords do provide us with a great deal of the information we need to compose, or improvise, a bass part.

For now I'm going to introduce you to the concept of how chords are created in any given key. The most basic chord is known as the triad, which is a chord made up of three different notes. Chords are built by taking every other note of the scale. So if we're to create a chord of C, we start with C (this note now becomes the ROOT of the chord), we ignore the next note of the scale (D) and choose the following note - E (this note is now becomes the 3rd of the chord), we then ignore the next note of the scale (F) and choose G (this note now becomes the 5th of the chord). The names given to E and G in this example are easy to understand if you think that E and G are the 3rd and 5th notes of the scale respectfully. As shown in the diagram, each note of the scale can be considered as a root note and a chord constructed, by choosing the 3rd and 5th notes above this root.
If this process is carried out on all seven notes of the scale (key) you'll notice (if you play the chords) that

Example

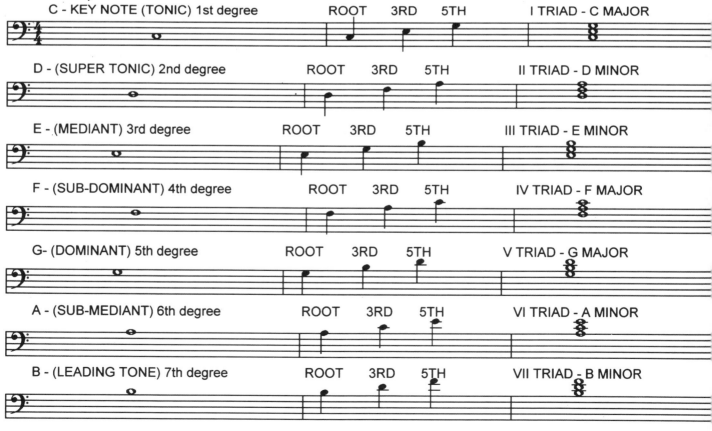

C - KEY NOTE (TONIC) 1st degree   ROOT   3RD   5TH   I TRIAD - C MAJOR

D - (SUPER TONIC) 2nd degree   ROOT   3RD   5TH   II TRIAD - D MINOR

E - (MEDIANT) 3rd degree   ROOT   3RD   5TH   III TRIAD - E MINOR

F - (SUB-DOMINANT) 4th degree   ROOT   3RD   5TH   IV TRIAD - F MAJOR

G - (DOMINANT) 5th degree   ROOT   3RD   5TH   V TRIAD - G MAJOR

A - (SUB-MEDIANT) 6th degree   ROOT   3RD   5TH   VI TRIAD - A MINOR

B - (LEADING TONE) 7th degree   ROOT   3RD   5TH   VII TRIAD - B MINOR they don't all sound the same. In other words the character of the chords changes. Sometimes the chord sounds bright and positive and other times the chord sounds melancholy. You are now hearing the difference between major and minor chords. So, in addition to having major and minor scales, with their respective characters, we also have major and minor chords, also with their respective and distinctive characters. You will also discover that on the seventh note of the scale a new name appears, the diminished chord. This is not a commonly used chord in contemporary music so for now we'll ignore it. (You can think of the sound of diminished chords as being 'heavy suspense' - you often hear them as background music in horror movies.)

You have just been introduced to how a key works - harmonically. The first note of the scale produces a major chord, the second note a minor chord, likewise the third note, the fourth and fifth notes of the scale both produce major chords, the sixth note a minor chord and as I've just mentioned the seventh note produces the diminished chord.

For the most part in this book we are going to concentrate on the three chords that are major, in the major scale. These chords occur on the first, fourth and fifth notes of the scale. These numbers (which are abbreviated to roman numerals I, IV, V) can be used to describe each of these chords. The advantage of using numbers is that we can discuss general points of music without having to talk about any key in particular, or any note. This should make it easier to understand that any point discussed using numbers to identify chords can be applied to each and every key.

These three chords are of considerable importance in establishing tonality. Tonality is the illusion of a key centre, or the impression that the key note is the strongest tone. By hearing a note as the strongest, we are also given to thinking that this note is the point at which the music concludes or is at peace. This peace is often referred to by musicians as release, all other chords in the music represent different degrees of tension. The concept of tension and release is played on in all conventional composition.

Try and play the following chords. IV and V.
One after the other they are never really at peace, the mind can hear in the 'distance' the I chord. If you

Example

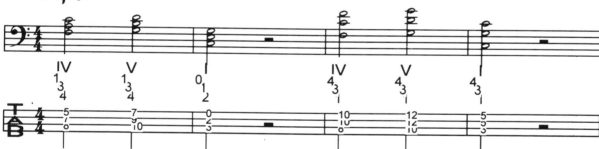

conclude this simple exercise by playing the I chord you will immediately feel at peace, as though that is the chord you've been waiting for all the while that the IV and V chords were playing. This illusion is felt by all of us and is principally the means of achieving both tonality - a key centre, and from this the ability to compose music with combinations of tension and release.

It follows that if these three chords alone can produce all this then why have other chords for music. The answer is of course variety and subtlety. On their own they produce effective, yet unsophisticated music. However, these three chords on their own are responsible for a great many blues, rock and early soul songs. They are often referred to as the Three Chord Trick - frowned on by some people because of their simplicity they are often seized upon by those less 'snobbish' musicians to create some very vibrant and even today some very original songs. The I, IV and V chords are also the three chords used by countless jamming musicians around the world forming them into the 12 bar blues.

12 BAR BLUES PROGRESSION:

Chord progression (numerical) | I | I | I | I | IV | IV | I | I | V | IV | I | V |

PLAYING & READING

You will have probably noticed from the guidelines given in Target - 1 for the earlier basslines that music notation only gives you the most basic information about how to really play a bassline. There is a need to interpret music that has been written down. One reason for introducing some of the techniques for achieving a groove at such an early stage is so that when you listen to bass players on records you can analyse how they're playing. A great deal of the knowledge you need to interpret music comes from the experience of playing and more especially listening to music and different styles of music. No musician will be a very good reader if they are unaware of the style of the music they intend to play. It doesn't matter how good you might be at reading notes and rhythm patterns. It is not my intention to go into any real detail about all the different styles of music and bass playing. If you understand what to listen for; accents, weight of playing, tone, articulation (precise length of notes) and various other technical elements that will be described later in this book, you can learn about different styles of music quite easily.

However, the composer or arranger can make some points of interpretation clear, by indicating the dynamic required in the music - volume of notes and phrases. Also indications about articulation of notes (note length) can be made. The following table lists many of the important and commonly used dynamic markings and marks of expression.

Bassline 9.

You will see that I have included a few dynamic markings and other marks of expression in this piece. In common with most basslines, the first two bars establish the groove. It is therefore quite common to see the word simile written after the main concept has been established. This as you'd expect means continue in the same manner. Every time you play the Bb at the beginning of the bar you slide from A. Don't think of yourself actually playing A, think that you're playing Bb and quickly slide from the 5th to the 6th fret. The feel of the first section is heavy and strong. As you are sticking to the bass string, tone matching is not too difficult. The bridging section beginning at bar 13 wants to be very taut, so keep the notes slightly shorter than written and play nearer the bridge than is normal for the A string. The final section beginning at bar 17 is the most tricky section to get the sound right on. The difficulty is the number of strings being incorporated into the same phrase and therefore matching the tone. It is further complicated by the use of open strings. It is probably better to avoid all open strings except for E and play the notes at the 5th fret instead. It has to sound much more fluid than the preceding sections, try to run the notes into each other, being careful not to leave notes sounding together.

Example

BASSLINE 9.

12 Bar riffs

In addition to Bassline 9, I have included some examples of typical 12 bar progressions.

Example

The first riff is a basic rock 'n roll type of riff. Although simple and predictable it does illustrate how often basslines draw from the notes found in the chords they are accompanying. This line uses root, 3rd and 5th one after the other in close position, an arpeggio. This is the simplest and most complete way to reflect a chord. It sounds very predictable because there is absolutely no disguising the simple chord reflection. More sophisticated bass lines add other notes from the key to create a more melodic line. Always try and spot the chord being reflected when you look at and learn a bass line. The second line is not so obvious in its reflection of the chord, however it is fairly clear if you look carefully. The first note is the root, the second is the 5th, the disguise being to descend to the 5th which always sounds less obvious and the third note is the 7th. There is a little chromatic link at the end of the bar. Notice how this link has to be modified when the chord changes. The third riff has been included to demonstrate how a simple riff can be easily developed. The first modification is in bar 4 where the 3rd and 4th beats concentrate on linking to the D chord in the next bar. Bar 6 at first looks quite different, but on closer examination you will see that it uses the same notes as the previous bar, except an octave lower. The last note is modified to give a 5th link back to A. Bar 8 changes beats 3 and 4 to link to the E chord. This bar looks very different, but the second note is actually as expected, only an octave lower, and the following notes do change the concept slightly but again are all about linking to the D chord. Bar 10 is the same as bar 5, the first D chord, except that from the second note on it is transposed down an octave. Notice how most of the development is motivated by the need to link into the next bar. This means that the intention is to keep the music driving forward. The main trick for development is the use of changing the octave of the original idea. This is one of the most used means of developing music. The beauty of the idea is that you don't have to think of a new idea as such, but to the listener the change of direction in the notes makes the riff sound new and fresh. This is an idea that you could start trying to use now. What makes it tricky to use at an early stage is likely to be lack of fingerboard knowledge. Try and develop your own ideas in this way, again experiment and practice will give you the knowledge you need to make your lines sound really sophisticated, whilst remaining musically disciplined and solid accompaniments.

Sight Reading

Beginning to read at sight is a daunting task at first. How can people just pick up a piece of music and play it without first studying it and piecing it together bit by bit. As with anything, there are techniques both in the way of studying the topic and for actually dealing with it in practise. And, of course, you need to start slowly and gradually work up to speed and level. Sight reading really can be quite easily attained, however don't expect too much too soon. As with the study of music and bass guitar in general you need to set targets in 1 monthly, six monthly and yearly targets. It is perfectly reasonable, even for beginners to be able to read real basslines - at the correct tempo - in a matter of months.

First of all you need to split up the reading of pitch and rhythm. You should also cross reference any reading targets with ear-training targets. Playing music at sight is very closely linked with ear training because if you don't develop the ability to 'hear' the music before you play it you will find it very hard to get up to speed. Bear in mind that the fingers will anticipate where they are going better if the mind is already 'hearing' the music.

1st Pitch exercise.

Place the hand in 2nd position and start with the exercises given here.

When you have done these follow the same principles and write out your own. Don't think about your writing too much just ensure that the highest note you use is mid C and the lowest note should be low G. The object of the exercise is to first; recognise scales in notation (very easy to see as each note moves from line to space to line etc., the regularity is also easily seen). When you are happy about the fact that you are reading scales, try and look at only the notes where the direction changes. So if the music starts on low C and moves up the scale to mid G, only read low C and mid G. If you've learned your major scale of C properly, the notes in between will 'look after themselves'. This ability to look for notes of importance and to ignore those notes that will 'look after themselves' is your first, and probably, most important lesson in learning to sight-read. For now, practise writing out as many exercises as possible, but keep everything in the key of C major, and don't exceed the range or position already stated.

Sight reading rhythm: Continuing the theme of starting off simply, all you need to be able to do for now is practise distinguishing between whole, half and quarter notes. The exercises given should be sufficient but write some more if needed.

Example

Finally, when you're satisfied that you can readily recognise scalar movement and whole, half and quarter notes, try putting pitch and rhythm together in a simple sight reading exercise. Before you make your first attempt at playing the following exercises get immediately into the frame of mind that you are going to go from start to finish, even if things go wrong. The most important part of the exercise is not to stop. Taken to extremes, if you play the first note in the correct place and the last note in the correct place, this is better than allowing the tempo to waver or worse still to stop completely. This is more difficult than it sounds because our natural instinct to play the exercise correctly takes over. For example, you make a mistake on the third note. Most people will stop and start again - Don't - keep going. Keeping the timing intact and keeping your place is your prime target.

Example

When developing sight-reading in particular always bear the above in mind. If you buy more books of bass lines (highly recommended) use a proportion for sight-reading study. Never actually learn these lines, simply practise playing from start to finish, keeping your place and timing together. Later in this book I will be showing you how to deal with, and indeed encouraging you to try and sight-read lines that are too difficult to read 100% correctly first time. However, for now be happy with your accomplishments thus far - you've established the ground rules.

IMPROVISATION & COMPOSITION

Developing riffs into simple song structures using the 12 bar blues format and other variations of the three chord trick.

By now you should have quite a collection of riffs and ideas. Your target now is to try and develop these ideas into imaginary song structures. One of the earliest and most basic song structures is the 12 bar blues. The attraction of it for now is that you should already know how it goes. Also it uses the I, IV and V chords, the three chord trick. This means that all the chords will be of the same type (Major - if the key is major, Minor if the key is minor). This in turn means that your riff or idea can simply be shifted without any need for modification to each chord location as you get to it.

Try it with your favourite idea. If this is centred around A, then your IV and V chords will be D and E respectively. To turn into a twelve bar song simply play your original riff 4 times on A. Then move the entire riff to the adjacent string, which will mean that it is starting on D, play the riff twice, then move it back to A and play it twice. Now move to the adjacent string and towards you by 2 frets so that it begins on E, play once, back to D, play once, back to A, play once and then back to the E, play once and then either conclude by playing a single A, or repeat the process.

The other experiment you can try with your ideas is to use the three chord trick to 'invent' an imaginary song. The three chords will work well with each other in almost any combination, and whilst this idea won't be very likely to give you a hit song formula it should give you the feeling that from your 1 bar bass riff a whole song can be formulated.

Think about the typical structure of a song:

· Intro.
· Verse
· Chorus
· Verse
· Chorus
· Middle 8
· Chorus
· Chorus

(A huge percentage of songs roughly follow this type of song structure or format.) Invent a chord progression, using only the three chord trick chords found in A. Namely; A, D and E. Invent a chord progression for your imaginary verse, an example might be: D | D | E | E | D | E | D | E ||
Next imagine your chorus : A | E | E | D | A | A | E | A || Then an imaginary middle 8 : D | A | D | A | D | D | A | E ||

This may or may not sound good for your riff, but it will give you a sense of having composed a song to some extent. (To compose a song properly implies that you have also created a melody and lyrics.) Also your imaginary song will help you to appreciate how long you have to maintain your riff and playing. If it was quite a busy line, you will feel the strain and this will help impress on you the need to develop stamina in your technique exercises. You may find it hard to maintain the tightness rhythmically etc. Of course the above chords are only an example, you should be able to mix the three chords at random and obtain acceptable results, although it will help if you take note of which chord is your release point and which ones create tension so that you can try and create a composition with a considered element of tension and release.

Pitch - the arpeggio, 3rd, 5th and octave.

When you have got really used to singing the major scale it is time to begin learning the sounds of intervals that are larger than the tones and semitones that make up the major scale. The first step is learn the major arpeggio. The word arpeggio is used to describe the notes of a chord played melodically or in sequence (as opposed to a chord, where the notes are played harmonically or at the same time). The notes you will sing are the root (1st note of your scale), the major third (3rd note of your scale), the perfect fifth (5th note of your scale), and the octave (8th note of your scale). For now don't worry if you don't understand why the notes in question have names like major third and perfect fifth, you will learn that when you come to Musicianship - Target 3. It is not necessary to jump to that section for now.

As before when you started to learn to sing the scale, playing the arpeggio on the bass first, and copying the sound can be the best way of learning the arpeggio. Your aim is to be able to immediately sing the arpeggio having only played the first note on the bass. As with the scale, the more used to it you get the more deliberately you should sing, so that eventually each note is being sustained for 2 - 4 beats, with a pause to 'hear' the next note before singing.

When you can sing the arpeggio, it is time to learn the intervals (sounds) that make up the arpeggio. The easiest to start with is the perfect fifth. The shape that is created when you place your fingers to play the first note of the scale and the fifth note, will always give you a perfect fifth. Begin learning this sound by singing the first note of the scale and then jumping straight to the fifth note of the scale. The interval or distance between these two notes that you have sung will always feel and sound the same irrespective of which note you call the first note. Try and change the starting note, perhaps move to the fourth note of the scale. Play this new note and see if you can sing a fifth above this. If you can't do this at first then use the bass to help you. Repeat the whole exercise. Play the first note of your scale and see if you can (unassisted by the bass if possible) sing the fifth note of the scale. Repeat these two notes several times (plenty of space between notes, though). When this starts to feel easy, play the fourth note of the scale again and try again to sing a fifth above this (this should bring you out at the octave, or eighth note of your scale). Once again when you have the notes in you head keep repeating them. The whole process may need a great deal of repetition and your may find that it takes several days before the voice and ear lock together to fully understand this interval. Do not rush this process. Learning your first interval is going to be the hardest, but once you understand how to pitch a perfect fifth above a note, you will easily understand how it can be done for all other intervals, in time. Before moving onto any new intervals, you should ensure that you can pitch a perfect fifth above any note you choose to play on the bass. (You will be limited to what you can physically sing, but you should be able to vary the notes sufficiently from day to day to know whether you are really hearing and understanding this interval.) Repeat all the steps taken to learn the fifth for the major third (1st to 3rd note of your major scale). Again the shape and fingering of this interval should be kept the same as you increase the random selection of starting notes. The major 3rd is more difficult than the perfect fifth when you introduce the random element to selecting starting notes. This is because your mind has got used to the key of your scale. If, by selecting notes at random, either the 1st note or the major third above it is off the original key then you can find yourself singing a minor 3rd, which is a semitone smaller. I find it a positive aid to learning interval sounds if you get used to learning specific intervals from any given note at random. However, you do need to be aware that constantly shifting the key makes the exercise more difficult. Try at first to master the major third when sung from the 1st, 4th and 5th notes of the scale. Then try and pitch from the 2nd, 3rd , 6th and 7th notes. In each of these cases the note you finish on will not be in the original key, and you may find this takes some getting used to. The benefit of trying, is that you are trying to learn the sound of the major third. Use the character of the sound to help you pitch the interval, this will make the key less relevant.

On page 44 are the 18 rhythm patterns which either individually or combined make up the vast bulk of all rhythms you are ever likely to hear or need. You should be aware that there are a great many more rhythmic possibilities, but it is surprisingly rare to find yourself needing to go beyond these patterns. Your first task is to learn to play patterns 1-8. You will find that some of the information in this section is repeated in the section on reading rhythm. The first part of the process of learning to recognise rhythm by ear is of course to learn to play the rhythms. It does help to sing or tap rhythm in addition to using the bass - although this is not essential.

For now concentrate on being able to play individually each of patterns 1 - 8. Start your practice of a particular rhythm with the drum machine or metronome on and spend the second half of your practice trying to maintain the accuracy with the drum machine switched off. It is important to realise that drum machines and metronomes should be used to develop your time keeping abilities. They are not there so that you can get lazy and let someone or something else do the work. Real drummers need and like bass players they work with to be equally strong time keepers - you should never expect the drummer to take all the responsibility in this area.

When you play each individual pattern repetitively keep the sound unbroken. For example pattern 4 is a single quarter note, so simply repeat each beat so that you are playing continuous quarter notes. With pattern 6, you have a two beat pattern, so repeat every 2 beats etc..

Example

An introduction to slap bass style.

Slap bass has always been one of the most appealing styles to bass players of all levels. Great fun to play even if you're on your own practising. By the end of this book it is hoped that you will be well grounded in this style.

For now it is my intention to just get you started. A good foundation on which to develop this style is essential. For now virtually all attention needs to be focused on the right hand - in particular the action of the thumb. As with conventional right hand techniques, the support given to the hand by the shoulder and arm will enable you to be most effective. Unlike fingerstyle technique, the forearm is used to position and support the hand. Place the upper forearm, just below the elbow, on the body of the bass above the bridge. Place the thumb on the E string resting on the last fret, with the length of the thumb parallel to the E string. The thumb action itself comes about by rotating one bone around the other in the forearm. Keeping your arm in position, practise turning your forearm so that the thumb rotates 90°, then turn it back. Repeat this trying to get the action to feel easy and loose. The main aim (technically) in using the thumb to slap the bass (usually the E and A strings) is to ensure that the forearm is able to rotate freely and easily. Don't twist the wrist as this will tighten up the forearm. The wrist should be relaxed at all times except for the moment of impact with the string when it should be momentarily tightened.

Your base position.

With the forearm firmly (not frantically) pressed and positioned against the bass, above the bridge, allow the elbow to move back slightly so that the forearm (and thumb) are now pointing very slightly away from the bass. If your forearm was as long as the neck of your bass your hand, at this angle, would be about 12 inches away from the machine heads. This positioning away from the bass will enable the thumb to naturally and easily bounce away from the string after it has struck. This is very useful. Over the years I've found that one of the biggest problems with this style is ensuring that the thumb, once it's struck the string, gets out of the way so that the string can ring cleanly. By positioning the arm, right from the beginning at the correct angle, you should avoid this sort of problem completely.

The thumb needs to strike the string cleanly, without touching other strings. Try and strike with the same part of the thumb, accuracy is going to play a big part in the success of this style. Strike with the bone just above the thumb joint. To ultimately achieve a good rich tone playing in this way the thumb needs to connect with the string quite hard. The force should not be created by banging with the forearm but created through inertia. By keeping the wrist loose, as you turn the forearm, moving the thumb outwards (towards 90°) and then quickly reversing the turn in the forearm, the thumb will be flicked back at the string with considerable force, without having to use much energy or muscle power from the forearm. You can of course get

Example

THUMB ACTION, REGULAR STEADY BEATS

OPEN STRING
USE RIGHT HAND DAMP

FRETTED NOTE
USE LEFT HAND DAMP

OPEN STRING
USE RIGHT HAND DAMP

FRETTED NOTE
USE LEFT HAND DAMP

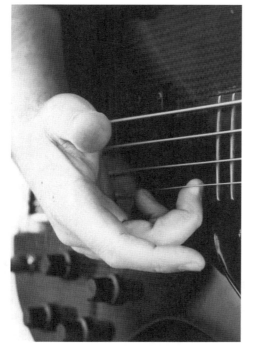

power from the forearm, but banging back and forth is both cumbersome and tiring.

Damping

The slap style can become completely unusable if you allow it to become messy. Don't put up with stray ringing harmonic sounds or any other unwanted noises. For now your main concern is to learn to damp with the fingers of the left hand, and with the base of the palm of the hand. When you practice striking the open E string or A string with the thumb cut each note short by dabbing the strings with the base of the palm of the hand. When you practice striking the E and A strings whilst fretting a note, use the fingers of the left hand to damp. Do this by taking the pressure off the string, but keeping at least two fingers (preferably all four fingers) on the string. Ensure also that the length of the first finger rests gently on all the higher pitched strings (D and G strings) to cover the risk of unwanted noise coming from these strings.

The Pop

The 2nd aspect of the slap style to introduce you to is the 'pop'. This is a variation of fingerstyle pluck where the string is lifted by the finger, vertically, just enough for the string to snap back onto the fretboard with a metallic snap to the sound. This technique can be incorporated into normal fingerstyle playing, but when used within the slap style the position of either the middle or index finger will be determined by the thumb's position. At this moment the thumb is aiming for the last fret.

This will put your finger between the end of the neck and the neck pickup (on two pick up basses). At this stage it doesn't matter whether you use your index finger or your middle finger to create these pops. Eventually, it is useful to be able to use either finger with ease. For now just use whichever finger feels most comfortable.

When making the pop roll the forearm with the same action that you practised with the thumb, rotating one bone around the other. This means that as you pluck (pop) the string, the thumb will

Example

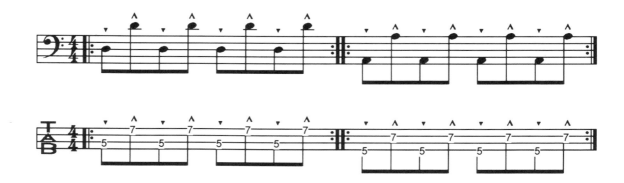

have come away from the bass 90°. The reason for doing this, as opposed to just plucking up on the string is that it will eventually enable you to play a following note on the thumb automatically as the thumb swings back into the string. This is important as eventually the alternation of thumb and pop can be very rapid. You should also find that it is almost impossible to get your finger 'trapped' under the string. Remember when popping the string that you don't have to rip the string out of the bass to create a powerful sound, just ensure that the string lifts vertically and that the release from the finger is snappy. The string will race back to the fretboard to create that distinctive sound. You should never break a string employing this technique, should this happen you are pulling the string out too far from the bass, which will not necessarily improve the sound or even make it significantly louder.

To get the hand of incorporating popping and slapping together the following octave exercise should give you an insight into where this style and technique is going in future sections. Remember that when you do this style slowly, which you must do to understand how it works, that it won't sound it's best. Don't worry, the action is what matters for now. It may even feel a little wooden, again don't worry. Eventually things will happen very fast in this style and so if you develop the right action now it will save you a lot of pain later.

Mark King; bass player with Level 42. It's hard not to think of the slap style of bass without also thinking of Mark King. Technically, he's probably the best, the fastest etc. Whether you like the result or not, his influence on the state of bass playing, especially in the UK during the 1980's, was considerable. I probably had a phone call a week from someone wanting me to show them how to play like Mark King.

Intervals

In music, an interval refers to the distance, or interval between two pitches (notes). This distance is measured in scalar notes, or alphabetically. For example the interval, or distance between A and E = 5th. This is easily calculated by counting through the alphabet, or up the scale of A. e.g. A - B - C - D - E five letters. The interval from C to E = 3rd, C - D - E three letters etc. This simple naming of intervals gives only part of the name of an interval, known as the general name. When calculating intervals, the general name should always be established first.

Before moving onto specific naming of intervals you may be wondering why bother - when are intervals used by working musicians?

Intervals will usually enter most musical conversations. Simple references are often made to intervals when discussing vocal harmonies, for example you may be asked to sing a 3rd above the main vocal line. You may have to accommodate a new vocalist in your band by playing all your songs up a 4th. In addition to these passing references to intervals in everyday musical conversation, intervals are also used to label sounds when training the ear. If you follow the section Ear Training then you will be required to learn what a 5th (and all other intervals) sounds like. Intervals are also important for understanding chords, we've already used general names to refer to the notes that make up a triad, the 3rd and 5th. As chords get more complex, intervals are used to understand and remember their construction.

Intervals - The Specific Name.

There are five terms used when describing intervals specifically: Major, Minor, Perfect, Augmented and Diminished.

As your knowledge so far about keys is limited mainly to the working of the major key, it makes sense to work out all interval names by comparing any interval to the major scale. Any note found in the major scale will either be called 'major' or 'perfect'. The word 'perfect' is used to describe 4th's and 5th's. The term 'major' is used for all other intervals, 2nd, 3rd, 6th and 7th. For example in the key of C major the interval from C to A is a 6th (6 letters), and as the term 'major' applies to 6th's this interval is properly termed, a major 6th. C to F is a 4th (4 letters), and here the term 'perfect' is used, so the full name for this interval is, a perfect 4th.

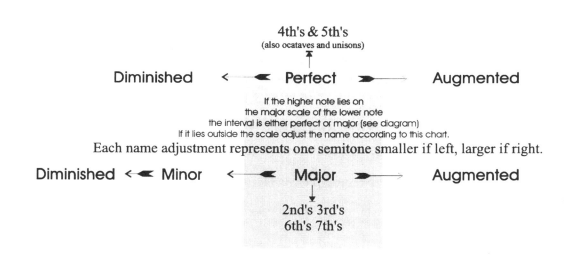

The diagram illustrates that when the 2nd or higher of the two notes being 'measured' does not belong to the major scale/key, that you adjust the name according to the diagram. So, 4th's and 5th's made larger by one semitone are called augmented. 4th's and 5th's made smaller by one semitone are called diminished. 2nd's, 3rd's, 6th's and 7th's made smaller by one semitone are called minor. 2nd's, 3rd's, 6th's and 7th's made larger by one semitone are called augmented. 2nd's, 3rd's, 6th's and 7th's made smaller by two semitones are called diminished.

Construction of common chords

Now that you understand intervals, it is possible to have a means of remembering how most chords are constructed, so that at least you will be able to calculate which notes make up any chord.

MAJOR	Root	major 3rd	perfect 5th	
MINOR	Root	minor 3rd	perfect 5th	
DIMINISHED	Root	minor 3rd	diminshed 5th	
AUGMENTED	Root	major 3rd	augmented 5th	
SUSPENDED (SUS)	Root	perfect 4th	perfect 5th	
MINOR 7	Root	minor 3rd	perfect 5th	minor 7th
DOMINANT 7	Root	major 3rd	percect 5th	minor 7th
MAJOR 7	Root	major 3rd	perfect 5th	major 7th

These chord types represent the most commonly used chords. It is not the purpose of this book to list every known chord. In addition to the above, it is common to add a 9th to any of the "7" chords (making 5 notes in all). Don't be put off by the name 'dominant 7'. This is actually the common 7 chord found in the blues sections in this book. If you learn these constructions, you will not find it hard to adapt your knowledge to all other chord types, as you come across them.

Important hand positions - concept and treatment for all natural notes.

Important hand positions are used to understand and learn how to play easily in a given key on the bass. So far we've learned the codes for the keys, and knowing the notes that make up a key of course plays an important part in learning how to play in a particular key on the bass. An important hand position is a position on the bass where you can reach 3 notes on each string from the key you've chosen to play in, within the normal hand span. This ideal is not always quite achievable, but it must be possible on at least 3 strings in order to qualify as an important hand position.

The real benefit of developing your ability to play in keys in this way is that you will properly learn the fingerboard. Knowing the fingerboard absolutely and totally sub-consciously is a fundamental requirement to being a true musician and bass player. Using important hand positions will greatly advance your abilities towards this ideal. The purpose of discussing important hand positions in this section is to deal with the process of learning the key and the actual position. You need to ensure that you look under the Improvisation and Composition sections as the exercises such as the variable triad exercise are conducted using important hand positions.

To start with you must understand the key of C major, or where to find all the natural notes. In this regard bass players are at a huge disadvantage compared to keyboard players as all their natural notes are easy for all to see, they are the white keys on the piano. Thinking of this comparison it is suddenly apparent that learning notes on a bass or guitar is actually far more difficult than for the keyboard. However, I use the comparison because your target should be to be able to look at your fingerboard, and be able to pick out where your natural notes are as easily as if they were all painted white. I don't subscribe to any ideas of marking your fingerboard as you are really only postponing the inevitable day when you have to take the markings off. Just get stuck in to learning and it won't take long to achieve the goal.

Your important hand positions for all natural notes are:

- **OPEN**
- **2ND**
- **5TH / 4TH**
- **7TH**
- **10TH / 9TH**
- **12TH**
- **14TH**
- **17TH / 16TH**

The first exercise is to learn where all your natural notes are in 2nd position. This will begin as if you are playing a scale of G major, however, when you reach the D string remember that you are trying to find all of your natural notes, not playing G major, so play F natural with your second finger. When you reach the octave G continue onto A on the G string, adding B and C. As you play both ascending and descending versions of this scale (don't worry what the scale might be called - it's not important) call out the note names. Constantly assess your degree of hesitation, there should be none whatsoever. Next, making sure that you always play notes with the correct finger, pick out (natural) notes from this position at random, identifying the note as you play it. Or test yourself - where is mid A? for example. Over a period of days (or weeks) depending on your practice level gradually get to know each important position. You don't have to master the positions before moving onto the next one but don't rush and give yourself too much to learn in one go either.

To enhance your study of important hand positions, check out the variable triad exercise in the section Improvisation and Composition - target 4

Example

Pitch recognition: *The 5th and octave.*

In developing your ability to read pitch, you will learn to recognise each interval in turn. This process cannot be rushed as it needs to be combined with an ability to hear these intervals also (see Ear-Training targets). If you succeeded in being able to easily read scales and the changes in direction of scalar passages in the previous target you will appreciate that part of the process that has made that possible is knowing instinctively which finger plays a given note of the scale. This finger automation is important to sight reading, especially early on. Be totally 'literal' with your fingering as discussed in Musicianship -Target 3 on important hand positions. Do all your sight reading in 2nd position for the time being.

The first interval to get to know is the octave. You will easily appreciate the distance between notes on the staff that are an octave apart. Fingering octaves is quite easy, but remember there are two basic shapes when fingering octaves. The common shape is a 2 fret gap with the lower octave on the 3rd or 4th string and missing out a string the higher octave is on the 1st or 2nd string respectively. Usually you would finger an octave in this shape with the 1st and 4th fingers. In sight reading keep the fingers on their precise frets, whatever position you're in, for example if you have low C to mid C, play low C with the 2nd finger and the mid C with the 4th finger - when sight reading. The importance of this is that you will keep the shape of your hand. Remember that in sight reading you have little or no opportunity to look at your hands whilst playing so relying on the shape, and therefore the knowledge that the correct finger is always near its respective fret is of great comfort. The other less common shape for playing octaves is from the E string to the G string, here the 4th finger always plays the lower note and the 1st finger always plays the higher note. In 2nd position this only occurs on 1 octave set namely, low A to mid A. So although this shape is less common it is extremely useful, especially in sight reading.

Before really putting octaves to the test, research all possible octaves in 2nd position. G-G, A-A, B-B, C-C. If this doesn't seem too difficult then you're right. Only four to learn, make sure you establish the exact fingerings for each and then you are ready to mix octaves with scalar sections. Use the following as examples and then write out a few of your own. Remember you are trying to develop an automated response. You recognise the octave written in the music, you 'hear' the octave and the correct fingers automatically prepare themselves to play. You don't need to consciously think what note the 2nd note of any octave pair is, always cut out unnecessary conscious thought.

Example

NOTE: When sight reading octaves use the literal fingerings for your current hand position

Next repeat the process used for octaves using the 5th. Again an easy interval to spot on the page, the fingering shape is virtually the same as for octaves. The only difference is that there is no string missed out on the common shape and only one string missed out on the second shape. In 2nd position you have 7 fifth pairs to learn.

Make sure that you are equally at home with octaves and 5th's descending as well as ascending. The shapes are of course the same, but hearing can be more difficult which can result in the sight reading being put off by this uncertainty.

Rhythm: 8th note pairs mixed with ¼ notes and ½ notes.

Example

PERFECT 5TH

SPACE TO SPACE
or LINE TO LINE

Basslines 10 - 16

A series of short sequences. Short sequences are an excellent opportunity to work on consistency. (Watch out for the key signatures, as most of the lines are in different keys.) Bassline 10, is a solid rock type of bassline, keep the notes well weighted and even, in the second bar the 3rd beat is anticipated so play this off-beat with the same weight as an accented note. The final bar is a little test to see if you can really move that 3rd finger - across to G, while your 4th finger is still on low Bb. Bassline 11 is a two bar concept, with the first bar on the beat and the second bar (with the exception of the first note) all on the off beat. I have written out the counting on this one as you're unlikely to get this right at first without being able to accurately control your counting. Feel-wise, try and keep notes on the beat slightly weightier than notes off the beat, but otherwise, very even. Bassline 12 is quite straightforward except for the slide and jump needed from the left hand to firstly slide to G, (this slide begins on F, a tone below). Bassline 13 is the kind of bassline that beginners find hard. This is because basslines with lots of rests, that stop and start, test your counting ability to a much greater extent than lines that just keep moving. I include the counting. Make sure that the rests are clean. The overall feel of the piece is quite light, almost funky so the notes can all be kept on the short side. Experiment with tone, especially on the short Bb at the end of bars 1 and 3. Notice that there is a staccato mark on these notes requesting specifically that you cut the notes shorter than written. Basslines 14 and 15 are both intended to really make you count positively. They are not hard if you do this. Try and avoid the counting and you'll never play them well. They want to go quite a bit slower than the previous riffs. Bassline 16 is made somewhat tricky by the position changes needed from the left hand. When practising position changes, look at the position of the whole arm. Look at the arm's position in 7th position, where you begin playing, and then look at the position when moving the arm away from you to play the second bar. If you understand the position of the arm and practice the required movement, then the fingers will have no problem getting onto their respective notes. It is a difficult riff to get good tone matching. The feel wants to be very smooth and even, this is hard when you are playing on every string and varying the hand position. The right hand will have to work at finding the right sounds for every note.

Example

OCTAVE STUDY

The octave study.

The secret of good octave playing (finger-style) is to match the higher and lower octaves for tone and level. Less experienced players usually have a great imbalance in the level of the higher and lower octaves. The commonest mistake is to play the higher notes much too loud. High notes cut through better than low notes, so even when you physically play octaves with the same force you will get an imbalance. Play the higher notes more softly than you would expect. Always the best way to achieve a good balance is to listen, really listen to the sound coming out of the amplifier. It is very easy when playing bass to assume that because the sound is amplified, there is very little you can do to control the sound, and therefore sub-consciously switch off a complete listening process. There is a great deal that you can do to control sound with the fingers of the right hand and if you care about the sound you make and experiment frequently with tone and level, you can soon be in control of the sound you make. The ultimate test is to record yourself playing as often as possible. You don't need sophisticated recording equipment, a humble cassette recorder will do.

Because of the nature of playing octaves the left hand has to be constantly shifting position. As has been stated previously, the position of the whole arm is the key to getting this right. If the arm finds the correct position and angle, the fingers will easily find their notes. When you understand the left arm movements, practice moving from the various positions required in this study without looking at the bass. This will get you used to the idea that even when shifting position, you don't really need to look at your hand the whole time. Even if you do decide to look when making position changes your confidence will be improved if you have done some practice without looking at the left hand.

Work at maintaining the technical accuracy of the right hand. Index finger on higher notes and middle finger on the lower octave.

Example

Improvisation.

Improvisation can almost be defined as knowing what note you're playing - and why you're playing it. Of course improvisation, ultimately, provides a vehicle for us to pursue our artistic goals and take us to a higher intellectual plain - honest! But it will be a while before you worry too much about that. It is the purpose of this book to give you the means and the technique to use improvisation for whatever purpose you wish. If you can understand how it is done, then you can take it to whatever level your ambition and ability to work hard allows.

To be a good improviser you need knowledge, lots of knowledge - about chords, keys and your instrument in general. You need technique so that you can do what your ears and brain are asking, and you need good ears. Your hearing needs not only to be good at interpreting what is in your mind, but more importantly needs to understand the sounds coming from the other musicians. Improvisation is rarely a solo effort.

And yes! You do have to start slowly - very slowly. The main point I would like to make before you begin trying to improvise is that you are trying above all else to develop your mind. The ability to think while you are playing, to create while others around you are also creating. Improvisation is primarily an intellectual skill. To begin studying, you need a vehicle on which to improvise, a composition. The easiest and most familiar composition at this stage will be a 12 bar blues. The 12 bar blues for all its familiarity and simplicity actually sets up quite a number of challenges for the improviser. At the end of this book you should be ready to try improvising on any chord changes, but for now stick to the blues and for now stick to the G blues.

The chord progression that we will use is as follows: (note that the second bar has changed from the simple blues that has been used elsewhere in this book. This is to make the study a little more challenging.)

|| G7 | C7 | G7 | G7 | C7 | C7 | G7 | G7 | D7 | C7 | G7 | D7 ||

It is very important when improvising to know the chord progression inside out. To help you attain this, learn the chords as bar numbers, so that, for example, you identify the fourth bar as; bar 4 - G7. You will appreciate this when the going gets tough. Basically be warned that as you develop your skills in improvising you will find yourself handling masses of information in a very short space of time. Knowing basics, such as the chord progression very well indeed, will help a great deal.

Next you need to know the chords. Again you need to really know these chords. If someone asks you what notes make up a chord of G7 and your answer is something like "Um err G um um er B and something else", then this will not be good enough for improvisation. There must be no hesitation in your thinking. In addition to the answer to this question rolling off the tongue as an instant G - B - D - F you should be able to turn the chord inside out. Do you immediately know what the 5th of G7 is (D), do you know the 7th of C7 (Bb) etc.. When improvising, this information is needed by your creative brain immediately. The information must be learned and re-learned so that it lodges deep in your sub-conscious where it can be accessed instantly.

Make sure you cross-reference this section with Ear Training and especially Musicianship. The following details on the chords is explained additionally in **Musicianship - target 3**.

G7: G - B - D - F
C7: C - E - G - Bb
D7: D - F# - A - C

In addition to knowing the chords with the notes in order; root, 3rd, 5th, 7th make sure you can always identify the 3rd, 5th and 7th of any chord in isolation.

You may have noticed that these three chords, whilst looking like a simple 12 bar using the three chord trick, contain key changes. You can easily see this by comparing the G7 and D7 chords. The G7 contains F natural and D7 contains F sharp. G7 contains B natural and C7 contains B flat. This has come about because of the addition of the 7th to all of these chords. However, it is the character of the blues that demands these notes be added. For our purposes it raises the stakes and increases the challenge very nicely.

G7 retains all of the characteristics of the typical I chord and the other chords retain their IV & V status respectively. So practically speaking we still have a typical three chord trick, but with the addition of subtle key changes. The key changes are subtle because if we take G7, we notice that this chord fits into the key of C major (the notes are all natural - F and B being especially relevant). The key signature applied to the C7 chords is 1 flat, and to the D7 chords 1 sharp. When keys change with very few note changes they are said to be closely related keys as they have many (six in the G blues) notes in common.

For now it is sufficient to think of each key as having an associated key signature:
G7 = ALL NATURAL NOTES
C7 = KEY OF 1 FLAT
D7 = KEY OF 1 SHARP

In Target 3 - Musicianship, the concept of Important Hand Positions is discussed. It is essential to work strictly within these important hand positions when first learning to improvise. Nothing will improve your knowledge of finding notes on the bass like it and nothing will improve your knowledge of keys better. Learn one position at a time because although you will feel restricted by playing in this way, it need not take long to learn each position and you will develop absolute knowledge of the key and fingerboard.

The first exercise is to play the scale 'forced' on you by the position you are choosing to learn and the key. For now, ignore the key changes of 1 sharp and 1 flat found in the G blues (these will be dealt with a little later) and concentrate on finding natural notes.

2nd position: G - A - B - C - D - E - F - G - A - B - C. There are eleven notes to learn. The exact fingers should, for now, always be used. Call out the note names as you play them. Then test the notes at random, your speed and lack of hesitancy when answering is a clue to your standard. There should be no hesitation or doubt.

The above exercise will give you a reasonable grounding in where to find your notes. Next you need to have some ground-rules before you set about trying to improvise around a composition. I have always used the phrase Reflect & Link with my students when describing the bass player's role in improvisation (and composition). The word 'reflect' suits the role of the bass player as guardian of the harmony (chord structure) of the composition. As a non chord player the bass player must look after the harmony by selecting the right notes from each chord to 'Reflect' the important sounds of that chord. The word link is a little more obvious, there is a need to join chord changes together hence the word link. So there are two principle roles of the bass player to understand. There is more that the bass player can provide, even when improvising an accompaniment. There is melody and counter-melody, the bass player has to understand how to create atmospheres and moods, how to encourage the top line players to pursue their goals etc. However, the early stage of improvising an accompaniment revolves around Reflect and Link.

Reflecting a chord is not as restrictive as simply playing root followed by 3rd followed by the 5th. This simple arpeggio will of course very adequately reflect a chord but it is not necessary to be this literal all of the time. A good 'ground-rule' is to think that you must always have at least 2 notes from the chord in strong positions within the bar. For now this means that the root will be on beat 1 and on either of beats 2, 3 or 4 there must be either the 3rd, 5th or 7th. Your choice of note(s) ultimately depends on what is going on around you. As a guideline, if the soloist is going mad and there is complete mayhem, your role might be the voice of reason, solid simple playing, holding the harmony together by strong reflection of the chords such as Root - 5th - 7th (link). You might decide that the basically major characteristic of the chords is being lost and therefore by using the 3rd frequently you can redress this imbalance. You might use the 7th frequently if you think that the sound is getting a bit tame, the 7th will usually help to introduce a bit of aggression into the sound, and will help the overall blues quality too. Having said this, your early goals will be practising for the time when you are improvising with others. In this book your target will be simply attaining enough knowledge of the chords, keys and fingerboard to make correct and genuine improvisation possible. Your aim is to understand each note that you choose to play. At its most basic, this means that if you are dealing with a G7 bar and you use B on the 3rd beat, you do so knowing that it is the 3rd of G7 and helping to reflect the G7 chord. You also choose the note because you understand the sound of the 3rd and understand the influence exerted by this note on the effect of the whole bar. These points are not hard to understand, but it does take time and a lot of practice before you can control and understand all the notes you choose to play.

The link: The means by which you move from one chord to the next is almost unlimited. However, as an improviser you should be limited by what you actually know. You must understand any linking structure by the effect it has upon the music. For the time being, I am going to introduce you to only those linking notes and structures that create a feeling of forward motion. This is the most common type of link, logically it is most common for the music to keep moving forward, as opposed to stop / start effects. The illusion of forward motion is basically achieved by enabling the listener to easily anticipate where the music is going. The easiest example to illustrate what I mean is to play C, D, E, F#, G. If, when you play this simple scale, you pause on the F# you will be almost aching to hear the G, which naturally concludes the phrase. In this structure, as soon as the scale begins with C, D, E the listener is being drawn towards the scale's conclusion. When the scale moves to the F# the listener's desire to hear it reach its conclusion is very strong and when the G is finally played the listener is totally satisfied by this logical conclusion. This example uses two devices to create forward motion, the diatonic (major) scale and the leading tone. Either one of these will create forward motion, and when combined is very powerful.

There are really two types of link; the scale link, of which there is really a basic choice of either diatonic or chromatic, and the 4th beat links.

The 4th beat links are:

1. **The Leading Tone** - a semitone below each root in the blues. The leading tone is actually the 7th note of the major scale. Use of a leading tone makes a statement that the following root note is also the key note. In a blues this is basically true as the key does in fact change when the chord changes.

2. **The Blues Third** - A minor third resolving to a major third. Is derived from the way 3rd's were treated originally by blues singers. They begin the note slightly sharp of a minor third and bend the note towards the major third. A good impression of a true blues 3rd can easily be achieved on a fretted instrument by sliding from the minor 3rd to major 3rd (see basic fall back exercise for examples. The blues 3rd creates a tension in the sound that is best resolved by the root of the chord, and as a result works well in creating expectation in the listener and therefore forward motion.

3. **The Fifth** - The powerful way of announcing a root note. This sound does not create quite such obvious expectation in the listener as a leading tone or blues 3rd, however, it has such power when resolved that the flow does not appear interrupted. Whenever discussing links, the link name is in reference to the chord you are linking to. So if you are playing from G7 to C7 and decide to use the leading tone as a link, then you are considering the leading tone of C which is therefore B. If, assuming the same chord change, you decide to use the fifth, then you mean the fifth of C which is of course G.

Scale links are easy to achieve. The word diatonic can be used as a general description of any scale that runs alphabetically. So all major and minor scales are diatonic as are the modal scales. Chromatic scales use all the semitones, all the frets and a chromatic interval is one where the note name is the same such as G to G#.

Any sequence of three or more consecutive notes constitutes a scale. So to create a scale link there must be three notes (including the root of the new chord) to describe the link as scalar. There can of course be more than three notes. Scale links can also ascend and descend.

The basic fall back exercise: This is an exercise designed to get you started on improvisation. One element of improvisation that players of all levels need, is time to think. It is usually necessary to have some simple playing techniques to enable you to take stock of the situation and plan your next move. As you get better at improvising, your plans would be for longer and longer periods. At the beginning you should be quite satisfied if you can genuinely plan the next bar. To do even this seemingly simple task you will need to have a way of playing that can be accomplished automatically. This is the aim of the fall back exercise, to provide you with simple structures, that can be used either when you are under pressure and need to 'buy time' to recover, or if you want time to plan the next bar. The method used to reflect the chord is always the same, so there is not much that is improvised at this stage, however, you will be trying at the end of the group of exercises to mix the three types of 4th beat link; leading tone, blues 3rd, fifth. This choice of links does mean that even with this simple exercise there is an element of decision making, and therefore an element of improvisation.

Example

Composition Exercise

The difference between improvisation and composition in this book is that improvisation is geared towards the techniques needed to create music spontaneously, and composition is for music that, for now at least, you have time to analyse and experiment with. When first learning how to improvise, you have to concentrate on thinking while you're playing, and on the chords, keys and where to find the right notes. It is not practical to get too involved in the compositional integrity of your improvised part until these skills are acquired.

In composition the integrity of the composition is, of course, everything. You can use the information learned in composition to improve your improvisations and of course the common sense approach to chords learned during the improvisation sections can and will be used when working on your more considered compositions.

The example exercise is a model song, using a standard structure. The chords, keys and format are very typical of pop and rock songs and are designed to use keys and chords used elsewhere in this book.

For now get to know the chords for this model song;

Verse	‖ Am	Am	F	E7 ‖
Chorus	‖ C	F	G	C ‖
Middle 8	‖ Dm7	Bb	Dm7	Bb	Dm7	Bb	Dm7	Bb	Dm7	E7‖

The structure or format will go:

1. Chorus (As instrumental intro.)	x 2	8	bars
2. 1st Verse	x 4	16	bars
3. Chorus 1	x 2	8	bars
4. 2nd Verse	x 2	8	bars
5. Chorus 2	x 2	8	bars
6. Middle 8	x 1	8	bars
7. 3rd Verse	x 2	8	bars
8. Chorus 3	x 2	8	bars
9. Chorus 4	x 1	4	bars

You should always endeavour to learn the structure of a song and commit it to memory. You should, of course, always know and remember the chord progression for each section of a song.

To complete your target, you must now work out the notes that make up each of your chords.

Chord List

Am	=	A	C	E	
F	=	F	A	C	
E7	=	E	G#	B	D
C	=	C	E	G	
G	=	G	B	D	
Dm7	=	D	F	A	C
Bb	=	Bb	D	F	

The information contained in these chords is very important. It is this information that will tell you what key the music is in and therefore what notes are going to be available to you for composing or arranging your bass line.

Pino Palladino; One of the Uk's best ever bass players. Known especially for his work with Paul Young and more recently Oletta Adams - his ability to create the most amazing, melodic lines - within a strict pop format is truly exceptional. The fact that this is also done using the fretless bass makes it even more special.

Pitch - the minor 3rd and the minor 7th.

Rather than learn all of the intervals that make up the major scale and then eventually learning the minor scale, it is better to learn those sounds that are most common to contemporary bass players. As so many riffs are based round the pentatonic scale it makes sense to learn the intervals that correspond to this scale next. The perfect fifth should now be known, so the next interval to learn is the minor 3rd and after this the minor 7th. If you have not already completed this target (3) for Musicianship and Theory - target 3, then you should do so before moving on. This will clarify the names of intervals as it will be confusing from now on if you do not understand how interval names work.

The process of learning the minor 3rd and 7th is the same as for the perfect 5th and major 3rd. A good preparation though is to practise singing the pentatonic scale.

When you are confident in both major and pentatonic scales, and the major arpeggio, perfect 5th, major 3rd, minor 3rd and minor 7th your training will be helped if you can find someone to play some simple phrases for you to try and recognise. You can do this by yourself if necessary, you can record the phrases, leave them for a few days and then play them back. For now, be realistic, don't expect yourself to instantly be able to hear and play back anything you hear on record, these are still early days. Restrict yourself to 4 note phrases. The following are examples of the standard you should be aiming for. They include the perfect 4th even though you will not learn this interval specifically until target 4. The idea of the 4 note maximum exercises should be continued throughout this book. Of course as you learn an interval you can include it in your recognition exercises.

These examples should be familiar from the riffs and pieces you've learned, either throughout this book or elsewhere. Completion of this target should mean that you have confidence in most of the common riff sounds. This means you will understand the individual intervals that make up the riffs and will also recognise the whole group of notes. Eventually, you will find that your fingers recreate the sounds you hear almost automatically.

Rhythm

You should now be able to play patterns 1-8 repetitively. Now consider patterns 1-4 as control patterns. These can be used with any of patterns 5,6,7 or 8. Do not for the time being mix the latter study patterns. Create 2 bar exercises mixing control patterns randomly with one study pattern. Build the exercise up 2 bars at a time, so increasing the variation. The following examples should get you started, but write more and more until you are really *hearing* these rhythms. Always ensure that your foot is tapping and that you are aware of the beat number and of the eighth note sub-divisions. As you get better at rhythm try and ensure that your body feels loose and at one with the beat. If you are still stiffening up when you play time, don't worry - but keep trying to relax. As this section is primarily concerned with your ability to recognise rhythm rather than read it, try and put your hearing to the test. If you have a friend that can tap or play a rhythm for you to try and recognise so much the better. However, you can quite effectively use records. When you listen to a record think whether any of the rhythms being played, usually by the rhythm section, correspond to the rhythms you've learned. If you think they do, stop the record, and tap out or play the rhythm involved. If you can tap your foot to this rhythm you should be able to confirm that it is one of the patterns you've learned. All of patterns 1 - 8 are extremely common. Often one pattern is used as the main rhythm concept of a whole song.

String crossing and arpeggios.

Crossing strings rapidly and/or making big left hand position changes are probably the most difficult techniques to master. The following exercises are an introduction to this difficult area. As with all topics begin slowly. With a technique that you know is going to take time to achieve, try and look into the future. What can you learn now that will last a lifetime? Balance is an aspect of technique to now take very seriously. You need to be able to move your hand and fingers around the fingerboard without needing to adjust the position of the neck and without forcing the neck out of position because of clumsy movement. With the string crossing exercises the speed you attempt the exercise affects your arm position. You start off with the hand correctly placed for the G string and end up with your arm correctly placed for the E string. In between, the arm position should be averaged out so that it moves smoothly and progressively from the start to end points. This will involve very minor compromises in finger positioning, but this is

preferable to any jerky movements that would otherwise occur if you tried to be too literal with your arm positioning for each string.

Slap: Hammer-on and lift off technique:

In addition to using the thumb and right hand finger to strike the strings the left hand can also play its part in actually sounding notes. Play a note with the 1st finger, anywhere, and then without using the right hand again, hammer the 4th or 3rd finger onto the fingerboard a tone above the original note. You should now hear that note as if you had plucked it with the right hand. The main difference is probably that this note is not as loud or controlled as you would like. In conventional playing, the hammer-on is often used as a lighter note, it can help bring a smooth sung-like quality to a phrase. It is rare to hammer more than one note in succession because the volume tends to fall away quite rapidly. In the slap style, hammer-on technique is taken to extremes. With practise the volume can be as great as a note played with the right hand. When developing hammer-on technique your early goals should be about developing power. To create a powerful hammer-on, the striking finger (3rd or 4th finger), must first pull away from the fingerboard (curl the finger back) and then hammer onto the string with as much force as possible. You will find that aiming for the finger tip (bone) will greatly help in achieving a powerful sound that has as much attack as a note played with the right hand fingers. The exercise is marked as half notes. This slow method gears everything towards the power of the finger hammering-on rather than drawing on the energy from the previous note. Try and allow the previous note to begin dying away and then make sure that the hammer-on is timed to coincide precisely with the beat.

If you can develop real power with hammer-ons they can enable you to create the illusion of very fast playing. Beginners are often impressed with the speed of slap playing, but much of the speed is possible because there are four ways to actually generate a note.

1. Thumb strike
2. Pop
3. Hammer-on
4. Lift-off

The Lift-off: On the surface the lift-off is basically the reverse of the hammer-on. Technically though it is quite different. To create a note with real volume using the left hand only when descending (usually a tone) you cannot just lift-off your finger, as the name implies. You have to flick the string as you release the finger. This is not too difficult until it comes to generating real power. Once again, put all your early effort into generating power.

Example

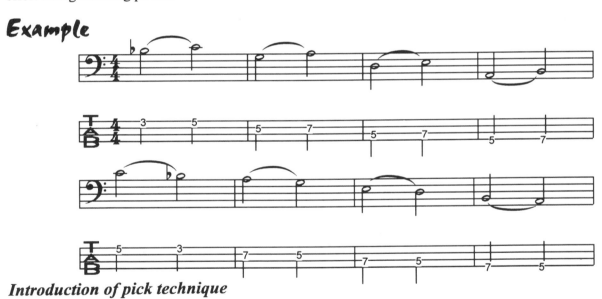

Introduction of pick technique

Before you begin taking up the pick as an alternative to fingerstyle, ask yourself have you time for another technique and have you made sufficient progress with your fingerstyle to take on board another technique. If you've followed the book through patiently then the answer should be yes but if not, postpone this section until you're ready for another technique or style of playing.

You can practise any exercise or piece that you've covered fingerstyle with the pick once you've overcome and understood the basic aims.

The pick, like fingerstyle, needs to be played firmly. The reason is completely opposite to the reason for playing hard with the fingers. For fingerstyle it is done to give attack to each note. The pick always has attack, but unless you play quite hard will lack bottom end - bass. Again, if you play firmly the note will be richer (contain more overtones as well as a more pronounced fundamental or main note). The electronics will also be able to achieve more if the sound is rich in overtones to make possible an even wider range of sounds.

The main objective for this target period is to establish your benchmark standard from which your own personal style will eventually develop. Initially the pick will comprise down and up strokes. These correspond fairly closely with middle and index finger in fingerstyle. In general you alternate down and up strokes. Begin on the G string. Grasp the pick between the index finger and thumb of right hand. Hold the pick at a right angle to the thumb. The thumb is then held parallel to the strings and sweeps in an arc across the strings. This movement is generated from the wrist, rather than from the elbow. The lower half of the forearm is placed on the body of the bass, above and behind the bridge. The pick needs to travel through the string maintaining it's shape. Don't at this stage allow the pick to twist or deflect upwards - it wants to travel cleanly through the string, and the sound should be clean and pure, no scraping noises from the pick. (When you understand the basics of the pick, adjusting the angle to create noise intentionally is no problem.) The pick will now have struck the string as a down stroke. Hopefully, the thumb is still parallel to the strings, not pointing upwards, bring it back (beginning the upstroke) towards the G string and rest it up against the string. Ensuring that it is at right angles to the string and flat against the string, sweep the pick back through the string, once again ensuring that it does not twist or deflect upwards. Now repeat, slowly, keeping the sound clean and strong and keeping the pick at the correct angle. The pick, as with fingerstyle, should strike the strings about 3 or 4 inches from the bridge when playing the G string, and 1½ inches from the bridge when playing the E string. With the pick though, this is important not just for equality of tone, but also for damping those strings that are not active. This is most apparent when playing the G string as you'll notice that the right hand is either resting on the E, A and D strings or is in a position to do so. If it is not resting on these strings when you're playing the G string then introduce this aspect straight away. Good string damping is a very important part of good pick technique.

Continue practising the movement of up and down strokes, slowly, spending a minute or so on each string in turn. As with the right arm in fingerstyle, the arm will move forwards and backwards from the shoulder to accommodate the different strings.

Example

Chromatic scale

The chromatic scale introduces the idea of extending your basic hand position. A chromatic scale is constructed by using each successive semitone. If you play 1st, 2nd, 3rd and 4th fingers, in order, on one string you have the beginning of a chromatic scale. In order to continue the chromatic movement you cannot simply place the 1st finger on the next string in the same position, as the interval will be a tone, not a semitone. Therefore you reach back with the 1st finger, allow the thumb to move back with it, and reach back one position or fret. As the 1st finger and thumb are now one position lower, move the other fingers to this new position and continue to play the fingers in order, adding the 2nd, 3rd and 4th etc.. Each time you change string you will need to reach back with the 1st finger to continue the chromatic progression.

Descending chromatically is the same principle except that you need to reach back with the 4th finger this time. If you've worked hard at controlling the amount of lift that occurs when you release your fingers you shouldn't find it too hard to persuade the 4th finger to move in the opposite direction to the release of fingers, which will be following the order 4th, 3rd, 2nd and 1st.

Example

The Chromatic Scale (Beginning on E)

Changing position by expanding or contracting the hand and finger swapping. Although position changing is something to keep to a minimum when playing bass, there are a great many bass lines where changing position from one part of the neck to another is inevitable. Sometimes it will be necessary to make a jump and block position change such as moving from 2nd position to 10th position. However, there are many occasions when you can change position safely and silently by either expanding or contracting the hand. You can even employ finger swapping to take over a note played by one finger with another while it is still sustaining.

The exercise used to develop this technique is as follows: play 1st finger on the 2nd fret, then play 4th finger on the 5th fret. While this note is still sounding contract the hand so that the 1st finger closes up on and eventually touches the 4th finger. When the 1st finger is in contact with the 4th finger press it down onto the fingerboard and then release the 4th finger. The note should still be sounding. As the 1st finger will be in between the frets (and therefore having to press too hard to make the note sound) slide it up gently until it is in the optimum position just behind the fret. Now let the rest of the hand settle in the new position, 5th position, and repeat the process, climbing all the way up the neck until it is no longer practical to continue.

The reverse is also possible, albeit a little more tricky. The extra difficulty results from having to 'make room' for the 4th finger as it closes on and touches the 1st finger, in order for it to take over the note without any break in the sound.

The thumb moves whenever the first finger moves. Try to keep its position relative to the position of the 1st finger at all times.

Example

FINGER SWAPPING EXERCISE

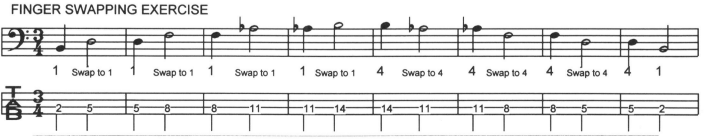

Key analysis

Chord symbols are generally quite a good way of conveying the main pieces of information about a song or piece of music. However, as a bass player, they only inform you which root note you can play, unless you actually know which notes make up each chord. Simply put, whenever you look at a chord symbol, e.g. C, you first of all automatically understand that this symbol refers to the chord of C major (not C minor which would be Cm) you should also automatically understand that it means the notes C-E-G. On this occasion you probably had all of the information just from the chord symbol C. The difficulty arises from the huge number of chords that exist. Getting to know them all takes time and effort.

When you are confronted by a chord progression, you have several chords, each containing typically 3 or 4 notes. These notes will give you information about the key of the chord progression. The notes will tell you whether the music is all in the same key or whether the key is changing at any point. To the experienced player this key information can be judged at the same time as all other information contained within a chord progression. To the beginner it is almost impossible to see which key the music is in when looking at a chord progression. The purpose of Key Analysis is to give you the ability to establish the key of the music from the chord progression.

Example 1. Chord progression = G - Am - F - Dm - C
Example 2. Chord progression = Fm - Bb7 - Eb - D - G7 - C7

Example 1:

1. Write out all of the notes in each chord

G	=	**G**	**B**	**D**
Am	=	**A**	**C**	**E**
F	=	**F**	**A**	**C**
Dm	=	**D**	**F**	**A**
C	=	**C**	**E**	**G**

2. Organise your notes into two columns, head one column "No Change" and the other "Missing or Change". Then, working alphabetically, look through all of the notes in all of the chords and determine whether any note changes, e.g. If there is an F in one chord and an F# in another chord then clearly F changes and so is placed in the "Missing or Change" column. If, as is actually the case in Example 1, A (natural), B, C, D, E, F and G are unchanged throughout the progression, then place all seven notes in the "No Change" column.

Example 1 =	**"No Change"**	**"Missing or Change"**
	A	
	B	
	C	
	D	
	E	
	F	
	G	

If, when you've analysed all of the chords, every note is accounted for and placed in the "No Change" column then the music has no key changes, and in example 1 has the key signature; All Natural Notes. 3. To determine the key name you have to decide which note/chord is going to be heard as the key note. As you know from learning about the 3 chord trick, the I, IV and V chords are likely to play a role in deciding this, as the interaction of these chords with one another always results in the I chord sounding strongest, and therefore sounding as the key note/centre. Of course the progression may contain more than three chords making it hard at first to see which chords are which. For now you only have to decide between major and minor, so you only have to decide if the key is C major or A minor. It is true in this example that you have Am and Dm which could possibly be the I and IV chords in A minor, but you have G, F and C major, which if you take C as the I chord give you F as the IV chord and G as the V chord. This states conclusively that the key is C major.

Example 2 = Fm - Bb7 - Eb - D - G7 - C7

1. Chords list;

Fm	= **F**	**Ab**	**C**	
Bb7	= **Bb**		**D**	**F**	**Ab**
Eb	= **Eb** **G**	**Bb**		
D	= **D**	**F#**	**A**	
G7	= **G**	**B**	**D**	**F**
C7	= **C**	**E**	**G**	**Bb**

2. More complicated than example 1. Notice that when looking at the chord progression, although the key is clearly a flat key, you wouldn't necessarily realise that there was a sharp key in there as well (unless you have learned to recognise all the notes in D major instantly of course). When you write out the notes of all of the chords, key changes are easily seen. It is still difficult, at first, to work out the keys from all this information, but when you get key changes in music, your first priority is to know which keys the music is in and where the changes occur. Your first job is to identify the problems, this means dividing into the two columns of "No Change" and "Missing or Change".

"No Change"	**"Missing or Change"**
	A / Ab
	B / Bb
C	
D	
	E / Eb
	F / F#
G	

The above analysis indicates that there are at least two key changes. This is because there is clearly a section that is flat and a section where there is one sharp. However, the above information is fairly limited at this stage because there could be as many as 5 different keys in this music. The music could be in 1 flat, 2 flats, 3 flats, all natural and 1 sharp. It is unlikely in practice that the flats are not part of the same key change, 3 flats. The next step therefore must be to determine where these changes are occurring. Looking again at the chord progression; Fm - Bb7 - Eb - D - G7 - C7 it is possible to group the first 3 chords together in the same key, 3 flats, but each of the other chords must be in its own key. D7 contains F# and so cannot be in the same key as G7 which contains F natural, and G7 contains B natural and so cannot be in the same key as C7 which contains Bb. So this music is in Eb major for 3 bars (II - V7 - I (conclusive)), then is in G major (1 sharp), C major (all natural) and F major (1 flat) all for one bar. The only other possible analysis is to put the D major chord in D major with two sharps (increasing the extent of the key changes). However, this is unlikely, partly because if you look closely you'll see that all of the last three chords contain, as their 3rd, the leading tone to the next chord. This is relevant because it explains the choice of chord, leading one to the other through the keys to get back to the original.

Thankfully most songs are much more like example 1 and so it should be a while before you have to get all that involved in complex key analyses. The main reason to analyse the key of music is to gather together all the information contained in the chord progression, so that you are always making your creative decisions based on the correct set of notes. If you have all the information to hand when you are arranging your part then you can be confident of compositional success.

Common chord progressions (major)

One of your most useful allies in music is that most of what you hear has been done many times before. You are already aware that the I, IV and V chords, the three chord trick, are responsible for thousands of songs. This makes recognition of these compositions easy. This also means that often an idea you've used before on a three chord composition will work again on another three chord song.

This section combines with ear training to provide you with the ability to recognise harmonic progressions.

The progressions that you need to know are:

- I - IV - V
- IV - V - I
- V - IV - 1
- I - IV - V - IV - I

The above are really intended to show some of the ways the I, IV and V chords can be combined. The following introduce the minor chords into progressions, although the overall key of all of the following examples is still major, notice that they either start or finish on I (major).

- II - V - I
- I - VI - IV - V
- I - VI - II - V

Learn the above progressions by heart and refer to the **Ear Training - target 5** to gain an insight into how to learn the sounds of these progressions and so develop an ability to busk.

> *Alembic: Originally made famous by Stanley Clarke, Alembic make some of the finest basses available. Exotic woods and even more exotic electronics mean that they are also amongst the world's most expensive .*

> *Anthony Jackson; Anthony Jackson is possibly the most widely respected of all bass players. This is due in part of course to his track record, from Chaka Khan to lesser known favourites of mine, such as "Casino" by Al Di Meola, which has got to be the sharpest, tightest playing ever. He is also known as pioneer of six string bass and is always recognisable when playing because his basses seem to resemble aircraft carriers more than guitars.*

Triple time riffs

There are three forms of notation used to indicate triple time. In all cases the feel and counting method is identical. Each beat divides into 3 and is either counted **1**-2-3, **2**-2-3, **3**-2-3, **4**-2-3 etc, or more commonly **1**-&-a, **2**-&-a, **3**-&-a, **4**-&-a etc. The foot tap is on the beat only (bold type).

1. The 'correct' method is to use a compound time signature such as 12/8. 12/8 time is understood as 12 eighth notes, which are grouped in 4 groups of 3. This means that 12 /8 is really 4 beats per bar, each beat dividing into 3 equal parts. In practice, this form of notation is usually reserved for music that is constantly varying the way in which the beat divides into three. The rhythm element assigned to the beat is the dotted quarter note.

2. The second method is to have a standard 4/4 time signature and whenever the beat divides into 3, a small 3 along the beam of the triplet indicates that the notes are to be played equally within the 1 beat. This method is usually used either, when most of the music sub-divides the beat into 2 or 4 with only occasional divisions of 3, or, when the music is made up of largely triplets and quarter notes or longer.

3. The 3rd method is to write the music as if it were sub-dividing into normal eighth notes and inform the musician to 'swing' the eighth notes. When eighth notes are swung, the second note is delayed to such an extent that it lies on (or near) the 3rd note of a triplet. This playing on the first and third notes of the triplet, **1** and **a**, is called a shuffle rhythm. This is the typical rhythm associated with blues and jazz.

The following example shows the same riff (which you can play as a 12 bar blues) in all three formats. Obviously the counting is the same. Be sure that you count an even three. The feel for triplets is in fact not totally strict timing. Musicians naturally play the note on the beat accented, and as a result this note tends to be slightly longer than the following 2 notes of the triplet. Don't think about this too hard, simply stress the beat a little and the feel will happen automatically.

Example

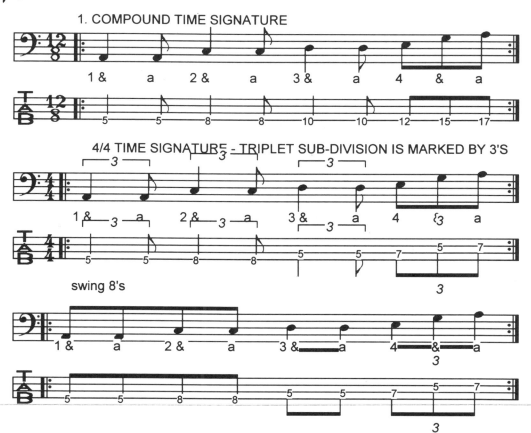

Example

As above, but written as:

Swing 8's

Example

SLAP STYLE

Reading:

The 5th and octave combination. There are probably thousands of bass lines that use the combination Root, 5th and octave, often as the only means of melodic development. A few thousand more use this combination as part of a more melodic structure. Either way, as sight readers we can be prepared.

In reading, as has already been discussed it is necessary to eliminate as much conscious thought as possible. Scales should now be read as a scale run from point A to point B, with only the notes at each point being thought of. When reading octaves you don't think consciously that both notes are for example low C going to mid C you just see a C and its octave. Likewise combinations of root, 5th and octave, just recognise the block of three notes. Fingering should always be 1st, 3rd (on the 5th) and 4th (on the octave). You can also easily extend recognition of this 3 note block to recognising a 4 note block (which is equally common) root, 5th, octave, 5th.

In 2nd position (C major) there are really only 3 locations to consider. Low G, D and mid G, low A, E and mid A, and low C, mid G and C. The B has been omitted because B - F - B contains a diminished or flattened 5th, which while not unheard of is much less common. Familiarise yourself with these locations technically and then mix with scale passages. An advance on this that can be safely added when the first exercise (plus your own) have been accomplished, is to mix 5th's and octaves to scales and root - 5th - octave blocks.

Example

Rhythm: Sight reading dotted rhythms
Example

Full reading, use the following as an example of standard. Generally, at this stage, if the melody is quite difficult (e.g. includes recently learned intervals and structures) keep the rhythm straightforward. If the rhythm is difficult, keep the notes to easily recognised scale structures. You need to invent many more exercises than those examples printed here to develop your reading skills.

Example

Variable triad exercise

This exercise is where the fun starts in improvising. You will now find out about thinking under pressure of time. An acceptable tempo for this exercise is 60 beats per minute. This means that you have 4 seconds per bar. In this four seconds you have to think about:

1. Where you are in the chord progression - bar number and chord name.

2. Which (chord) comes next.

3. Which notes make up the current chord

4. Which notes to select on this occasion

5. Which link to use going into the next bar.

Believe me, if your knowledge is patchy you won't think fast enough even at this slow tempo. If you have studied thoroughly then remember that you still should consolidate your knowledge so don't exceed 70 beats per minute until you have completed all the sections of this book.

The aim of the variable triad exercise is to strengthen your knowledge of chords and the fingerboard. Initially you will restrict yourself to the important hand positions. This is until you feel that all of the positions are known thoroughly - this is unlikely to be until you have finished this Level. In addition to this technical goal, the exercise will introduce you to the pressure of thinking while you are playing and will help you get used to handling a lot of information in a short space of time.

Reflecting the chord in this exercise is straightforward as the 'rules' of the exercise are to ensure that each bar contains the root, 3rd and 5th. You must also include a 4th beat link, either leading tone, blues 3rd or 5th. The exercise differs from the basic fall back exercise in the freedom you have to achieve these basic ideals. The root must still be on beat 1 but you can choose in which octave to play it (given the restrictions of the position you are in at any given time). The 3rd and 5th can be played in any order and on any of beats 2, 3 or 4. You can also choose in which octave to play them. Obviously you can only play a 3rd or 5th on beat 4 if it is also a link to the next chord, e.g. G7 - C7 you could play the B on beat 4, acting as both the 3rd of the G7 chord and the leading tone to C7.

To get used to the idea, research all the ways in which you can vary the triads, restricting yourself to just 3 beats (allowing for an easy use of the 4th beat link). On a four string bass, in second position, there are eight variations of a G triad, 16 variations of a C triad (provided you include open E) and 8 variations of a D triad. The following are examples of all of these variations.

I suggest you practise running over each of these variations before switching on the metronome or drum machine and playing the complete exercise under pressure of time. When you do begin the exercise, remember that you shouldn't repeat yourself within each 12 bars. The following is an example of non-repetitive use of these variations. DO NOT LEARN THIS EXAMPLE. Your playing must be different each time you play. Alter the variation you begin with, as this will generally ensure that the following bars are different. After a while, you will know instinctively all of the variations, keep trying to develop your mind all of the time, make sure that you know the note names and the role of the note (whether it is the 3rd or 5th etc.). The name and role of every note should always be consciously available at this practise tempo.

Example

Example

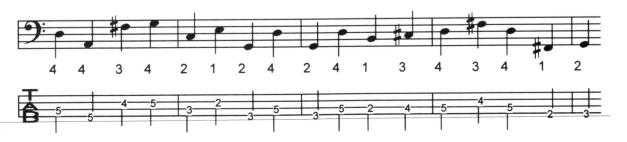

If you have managed to keep each bar different, and each repetition of the 12 bar different each time you play it using the basic variations then try adding the following idea:

Delay playing the 3rd or 5th of the chord until the 4th beat, for this to work the 3rd or 5th that you choose to delay must also be a linking note to the next chord. To make up the extra note, try duplicating any note of the chord. Playing the octave of the root on beat 2 is an easy way to get going, although eventually you could use any note from the Key! The following are examples of how to apply this idea.

Example

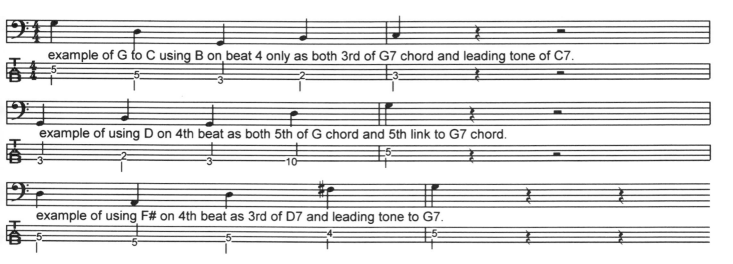

example of G to C using B on beat 4 only as both 3rd of G7 chord and leading tone of C7.

example of using D on 4th beat as both 5th of G chord and 5th link to G7 chord.

example of using F# on 4th beat as 3rd of D7 and leading tone to G7.

The examples on page 73 show how it is possible, even when restricting yourself to a single position, to create a totally non-repetitive bass line.

N.B. Always remember, that even though these exercises sound like an acceptable walking bass line, typically the type of bass line used by jazz bass players, the aim is not to learn how to play jazz walking bass lines that have real compositional integrity, but simply to learn the first lesson of improvisation, namely; to know which note you're playing and why. You should not be too concerned whether the whole 12 bars adds up to a really meaningful composition, what matters now is that you've learned the fingerboard and the chords to a high standard.

It is likely that you have so far only learned 2nd position. The variable triad exercise needs to be practised in each and every important hand position until you are totally confident in all positions. Don't skip the high positions as it is just as important to know parts of the neck that are used less frequently.

Example

EXAMPLE OF VARIABLE TRIAD EXERCISE IN 7TH POSITION.

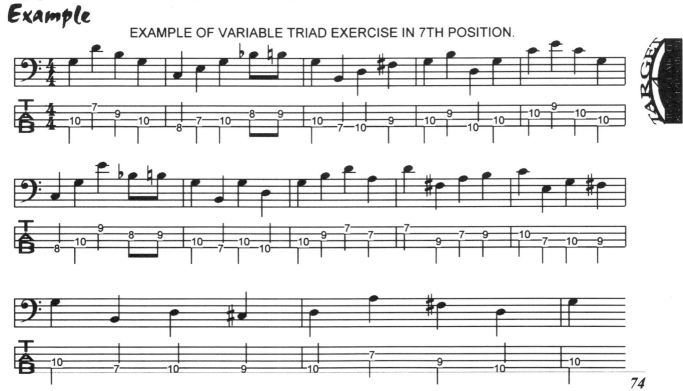

Reflect and Link writing

Reflect and link writing involves putting pen to paper (ideally) to explore what is possible when working to the 'rules' of reflect and link. This extends quite considerably what has been possible with the variable triad exercise. The main difference is that to stay within the 'rules' of reflect and link you only need have two notes from the triad. This leaves room for at least one note that need not be found in the chord, or part of the link. This note still needs to be chosen carefully as it can be used to create melody with the notes that you must use in order to preserve the harmony of the composition. It is not essential that you write down your ideas, they can be just be played, however you will benefit from developing a library of ideas which is only likely to come about if you write each idea down.

The following is the writing procedure. Stick to this procedure precisely and each bar will be technically correct. You are not guaranteed a brilliant sounding bar every time, however try to assess the potential application of anything you write, rather than dismissing some of your experiments as 'odd' or 'rubbish'. Of course the good ideas usually stand out from the crowd and should be written out again neatly so creating a library of ideas, which you should try and memorise for use in improvisation. Another use of each and every idea is as the melodic base for any riff. Try imposing a rhythm on some of your ideas, turning them into riffs that can be repeated and possibly even turned into a simple basis for a song.

THE WRITING PROCEDURE

1. Write the root of bar 1

2. Write the root of bar 2

3. Choose, research and write the link

4. Write the 3rd beat of the bar (unless your link is scalar when it will already be written)

5. Check whether you need any more reflect notes (minimum of 2)

6. Write the 2nd beat

7. Analyse the bar. Write root, 3rd, 5th, 7th as appropriate under the relevant reflect notes, and write which type of link you've used under the link. If you don't have at least 2 reflect notes and a legitimate link, then you need to make corrections as appropriate.

8. Play the 5 note 'composition'. Write down a brief description of the sound. e.g. Positive - mobile - angry etc. Try also to think of an application, the sort of song or music it might fit, or just be descriptive. Trying to describe musical sound with words may seem to defeat the object as music is really above what can be described in words, however, if you can think of descriptions you will remember the bar, and therefore benefit in the future from having composed it, . If you remember also how the bar was constructed, say it goes root, 6th, 5th, leading tone and has a generally good time feel, then you will be able to find that sound, know how to create it instantly, in any situation. This has great implications for rock and pop players who want to use improvisation to free up their mechanical bass lines. Again it is knowing what you're playing and why.

> *Nathan East: One of the most 'in-work' bass players during the 80's and 90's. He seems to feature on every other album you pick up. His real talent, I believe, lies in his combination of arrangement skills, great taste and, of course, great groove playing. My favourite examples are his playing with Anita Baker and Eric Clapton.*

Select a chord change

Choose the octave for the 1st bar's root note

Choose octave for 2nd bar's root (don't worry about the position)

Choose a link, eg leading tone

Write 3rd beat of bar 1. Try to choose a note that supports your chosen link

After checking whether you need any more reflect notes, write the 2nd beat of bar 1

ANALYSIS   Root   rpt root   melodic   3rd   Root

The link has changed from being a mere leading tone as was originally intended
by selecting 'A' on the 3rd beat, the link has become a Diatonic scale link.

The real aim of this exercise is to bury the principal of the writing procedure, the order in which you create improvised bars, deep in your sub-conscious. When the tempo is fast, no one really knows how they improvise, not in a detailed way, the very nature of the art is that it is dealt with sub-consciously. However, it is logical that the order laid down in the writing procedure must be fairly close. You must have a starting point (root of bar 1), you must then decide where you are going (root of bar 2), you must think how you're going to get there (the link), how best to reach the link (beat 3), check the harmonic integrity of the bar (beat 2). So by experimenting within this ordered structure you should, once you start really improvising, find that your ideas are technically sound, making it easier to gradually improve your overall compositional skill.

Continuous walking bass exercise

Now that you have the ability to easily reflect the chord - the variable triad exercise, and an understanding of how to use one non-chord tone to add melody to your bass lines, you need to start trying to use this knowledge to create music.

The continuous walking bass exercise can be done without any assistance. However, if you can either get someone to play the chords on guitar or keyboard, or if you can make a recording of the chord progression repeating several times (with a metronome or drum machine, of course) then you'll find it easier and more enjoyable.

76

The purpose of this exercise is partly to practise your variable triad exercise, without necessarily imposing the restriction of sticking to important hand positions, partly to see if you can slot in some of your favourite ideas from reflect and link writing, partly to develop the ability to really improvise, that is actually create a bar or bass line, as you play. Whilst practising for all of these skills, your aim is to always try and sound as though you're making music. You are already experienced at judging whether music is good because of your interest in music and your experience at listening to music. It is worth recording some of your efforts so that you can analyse them more closely at the end of each session. Don't worry about mistakes, they're irrelevant but concentrate your criticism on the musicality of your playing. Naturally don't expect too much too soon, and don't yet expect yourself to be able to really improvise. Conclusion of this target session is to give the impression to others that you're improvising by being able to play a controlled mix of variable triads, composed bars and lucky escapes using a G blues as your compositional base.

Song example - key analysis

Before beginning this section ensure that you have understood Key Analysis in Target 4 - Musicianship.

Chord List

Am	=	A	C	E	
F	=	F	A	C	
E7	=	E	G#	B	D
G	=	G	B	D	
C	=	C	E	G	
Dm7	=	D	F	A	C
Bb	=	Bb	D	F	

Key Analysis

"No Change"	"Missing or Change"
A	
	B / Bb
C	
D	
E	
F	
	G / G#

This analysis indicates firstly that the song does change key. It changes key at least twice, a flat section and a sharp section. There are likely to be at least three "key areas" in the song. The next stage is to determine where the changes occur.

You need to look at the individual chords and in what parts of the song these chords occur. The B / Bb conflict is quite easy to sort out. B natural occurs in G major, and E7 - chords that are present in both the verse or chorus. The Bb is only present in the Bb major chord, and this chord is only found in the middle 8. Therefore Bb, and the key associated with it is restricted to the middle 8. The middle 8 will need further investigation, but for now we'll call it Key Area 2. The other result of this conclusion is that B natural is present throughout the verse and chorus. Next establish where the G and G# conflict is occurring. G natural is found in G major (chorus) and G# is found in E7 (verse). At first glance you might now conclude that the chorus and verse are different keys. However, we can call the Chorus, Key Area 1 and we have established that Key Area 1 is an All Natural Note key. The verse, which we'll tentatively call Key Area 3, needs further investigation and care. If you've studied keys properly, you should be thinking that G# should not exist unless F and C are also sharp. A glance at your key learning chart in Musicianship - Target 2, will show you that G# is the third note to become sharp. However, you can see that the other two chords in the verse are A minor and F major. F major obviously contains F natural and both chords contain C natural. So for now at least, G# is contained within the E7 bars only. So Key Area 3 refers to the E7 bars. This means that the Am and F chords are proven to be in an All Natural Note key, and for now become part of Key Area 1.

Don't be alarmed if you find the whole business of Key Analysis a bit complicated. It is actually quite easy, the problem when you're a beginner lies in the fact that even though you've probably learned your key signatures, you don't yet have instant knowledge and therefore an instinct for keys. Working on key analysis will greatly help you overcome this, so if you haven't understood it yet, read again and cross-reference with your key chart until you see how the conclusions are reached.

EAR TRAINING

Pitch - the 4th.

You have already encountered the perfect 4th in some of the previous target's 4 note pitch recognition exercises. However, you now need to learn it thoroughly. The perfect 4th is the first interval that is difficult because it is actually quite rare melodically. It is not a very attractive interval either. The process for learning is the same as for the other intervals but be prepared for a slightly harder time with this one.

Descending intervals.

The 4 note pitch recognition exercises will also have introduced you to descending intervals. Up till now your studies have concentrated entirely on ascending intervals. Having now learned the perfect 4th this is a good time to get used to all the intervals learned previously, descending. Begin with the 4th. Really this is a far more common interval when descending. You'll recognise the following example as the bass line to seemingly every other country tune. **Example**

When intervals descend their name remains the same. This is logical as the gap between the notes, the difference in pitch remains the same. (N.B. Intervals are always named from the lower note to the higher - ascending.) However, the character of the interval is quite different. This is usually because the place within the key, or chord is different. The perfect 4th taken in isolation sounds like the root ascending to the fourth degree, which as stated before is melodically unusual, however the descending perfect 4th in isolation, always sounds like the root descending to the 5th of the scale or chord, which is a very useful and common bass line. (This sort of bassline will of course reflect the chord very well, and if the chord repeats, will also link effectively.) You may find that the perfect 4th is much easier to learn and understand, in either direction, when put in this context.

The 3rd's seem to have opposing characters when descending. The major 3rd descending (made famous by Beethoven's 5th Symphony) is very serious and very minor sounding. The minor 3rd descending is very light and easy on the ear (Hey Jude - Beatles).

OK so I've now started to give famous examples to help you recognise intervals. For some people this approach is very useful in simply learning and remembering the intervals. It is really more the case that as you recognise more and more sounds you realise that the opening notes of certain tunes use an interval that you recognise. If you are starting to recognise which intervals make up tunes you like, then you have begun to really understand sound. This sound will be easily replicated by you on the bass, as you will have been learning the fingering associated with each interval as you learn the sound. The connection between hearing and playing is now being established. There is much to do yet but if you appreciate these points then you should see how to move forward in this subject more easily.

Rhythm: Compound or triple time. Concept and basic patterns

So far the only form of sub-dividing the beat has been to count an & between each main beat, so dividing the beat into two. Compound time, which is more commonly referred to as triple time refers to when the beat is divided into 3 equal parts. The counting is typically 1 & a, 2 & a, 3 & a, 4 & a. When you count this ensure that each element is equal. You will then be counting triplets. A triplet is the name given to the group of three notes created in this type of sub-division. Usually the triplet is identified by the little 3 placed along the beam joining the three notes. (There are three ways that triple time can be notated, for more information on this see Reading - Target 4)

An introduction to busking. Busking within the 3 chord trick.

Busking is the art of accompanying tunes that you have never heard before or which you only know from occasionally having heard the song on the radio. Either way you need to be able to play effectively to music that you have not actually learned. To most beginners this seems completely impossible. However, you already know (from Musicianship - targets 2 and 3) that a great many songs use just three chords I, IV and V. You can probably already hear a 12 bar blues song and know immediately that it is a 12 bar blues using just these three chords. These three chords can also be used with each other in formats other than a 12 bar blues and they are almost as easy to recognise.

So busking is about recognising the type of song, the (chord) changes and being able to improvise an accompaniment (Rarely does this accompaniment have to be very complex - your approach will depend on how well you recognise the style of the music and therefore know immediately the right sort of bass line to apply).

The purpose of this book is to introduce you to the commonest chord progressions, so that you immediately recognise them. This is the most fundamental aspect of busking. The melody also gives clues and as your ability to hear more detail when listening to melody improves so will your anticipation of the likely chord progression.

To enhance your ability to really understand the sound of chords you need to once again use your voice. The complication when trying to hear chords and common chord progressions is that because of the variation in chord voicings, a chords character can be disguised. This disguise can be unmasked by singing through all possible arpeggio permutations of the chord progressions. This works by alerting you to the variety of ways that chords can be voiced, the order in which notes are placed in the chord. By familiarising yourself with most of the possibilities you will rarely mistake the chord type, and therefore rarely mistake the chord progression. The following is an example of the ways you can sing through a I, IV, V progression.

For simplicities sake, this example is in the key of C major. This may not suit your voice, however, you can transpose the example to any key by moving all the notes either up or down until it suits your vocal range.

Example

Interval scales:

Interval scales prepare the hands for the likelihood of playing backwards and forwards. Technically this tests the ability of the fingers to stay over their notes and minimise the finger release distance.

The example given here is for thirds, however this exercise can be copied with any interval.

Example

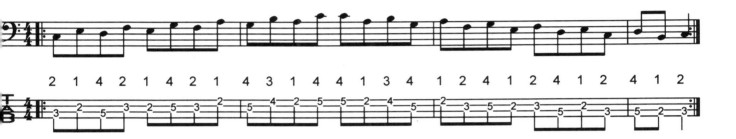

Dead notes in slap.

A dead note, sometimes referred to as a choked note, is a percussive sound, that should have no pitch (note) to it. In order to block any melodic pitch you need to rest at least two fingers onto the string. The touch here needs to be right. Touch the string positively and firmly, yet don't actually depress the string. This way no note can sound. It is a good idea when trying to block all musical notes to ensure that all strings are damped to some degree. This is because a string can vibrate even when you don't strike it or intend it to vibrate.

When played in isolation the dead note is not a very attractive sound. The more percussive and unattractive it sounds in isolation the more useful it is to the slap bass player when incorporated into bass lines. The following exercise will give you an introduction to the mixing of notes and dead notes to create rhythmically exciting possibilities. In any style of music and utilising any right hand technique dead or muted notes can be used to great effect. The technique is the same as for dead notes in the slap style. The degree of damping can be varied more effectively when using finger-style or the pick. With these styles it can sound attractive to allow some pitch to be noticed, creating a half-muted sound.

Example

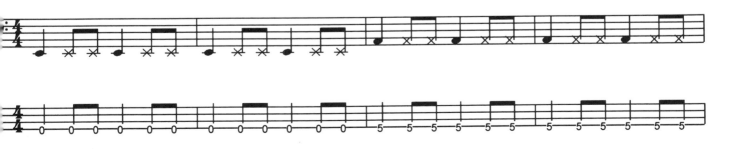

Right Hand Muting, when using the pick.

When using the pick, the right side of the right hand should be gently resting on any unplayed strings. This is an important damping technique. To mute strings with the right hand this technique can be exaggerated so that the right side of the right hand rests also on the string being played. This does force the hand to twist very slightly and you need to practise to accommodate this. By varying the amount of pressure used you can vary the degree of muting. The good thing about this technique is that a very slight mute can be achieved which doesn't obscure the pitch of the notes but does restrict the sustain, keeping the notes to a manageable length. This really suits the pick style. With practise, the pressure can be varied easily and instantly creating a wide range of sounds. Practise using any scales and stamina exercises that you have used for technique practise elsewhere. Copy the exercise for slap dead notes above, as being able to switch from full note to either full mute or half mute is a useful skill.

Stamina exercises; their importance and progress.

Although I've placed great emphasis on developing a technique that is efficient, bass is always going to be a physical instrument. You have to work therefore at developing considerable stamina. The faster you are able to play, the greater the demands on the muscles and the more you need stamina.

Before you begin taking stamina seriously you need to learn to breathe properly while you're playing. You may think I'm joking here but think about how you've been breathing up until now while you're playing. The chances are that while you're concentrating on some aspect of technique or other you are actually holding your breath, occasionally gasping air when the body tells you there is no choice - breathe or die. This is not good news for the muscles that have to move the arms and fingers. Imagine trying to run down the road holding your breath, you wouldn't get far and if you tried to repeat this gasping for breath every four strides or so you're legs would soon give up completely, starved of oxygen from this exercise. The main difference between running and moving fingers up and down on a bass guitar is that when running, your legs demand oxygen, i.e. make you breathe hard, whether you want to or not. There is no way you could keep your breathing normal even if you tried. Your fingers, when playing bass, could probably turn blue without the rest of your body taking the slightest bit of notice. In other words the small muscles that you use to play the bass do not demand oxygen automatically. So, you have to teach yourself to breath deep and hard while you are playing. It is a technique in itself and needs practising. The following routines for stamina exercises should always be practised in conjunction with deep regular breathing. You must take the muscles in your forearms and hands seriously, look after them, give them the oxygen they need and exhale fully to get rid of unwanted carbon dioxide. As with any form of physical exercise, the combination of rigorous exercise, accompanied by deep regular breathing will not just ensure that the maximum amount of oxygen is absorbed by the muscles but will in time increase muscle capacity (size), so enabling more oxygen to be absorbed. This in turn will allow you to play faster and for longer - which is the aim of this area of study.

The following exercises all follow the same format as 1-2-3-4 stamina exercise, where each string is played twice in each position and then the hand gradually moves up the neck one position at a time. The music example gives a few of the possible four finger exercise patterns. You would have to have a lot of practise time available to seriously practise all possible variations (there are 16 possible variations of 4 fingers) on a daily basis, so try and practise the following once or twice during each week's practise.

Example

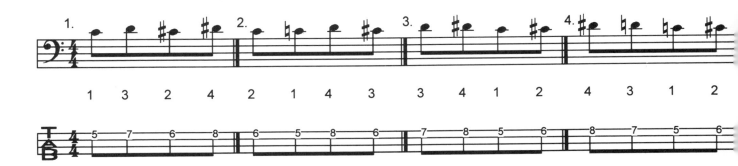

The minor key signatures.

You will now be aware that the vast majority of music you hear is either written in a major or minor key. Most music that is based on chords is written in this way. There are modal compositions, more often found in jazz and 20th century classical music, but these are much less commonly heard. As you have hopefully put in a lot of work to learn your major key signatures (codes), you will appreciate that knowing minor key signatures is as important. However, to get started on minor key signatures, learn first of all how to work out the relative minor of any major key.

The term relative minor, is used to describe a minor key that shares a key signature with the relative major key. First of all look at how the minor key, along with all the other modal scales, is developed from the major.

If, for simplicity, we keep all the notes natural and play from C - C we get, of course C major

· C - D - E - F - G - A - B

If you then begin on the second note of the scale and play (using only natural notes) D - D you get a scale called D DORIAN.

· D - E - F - G - A - B - C ·

This scale sounds almost like a minor, in fact it is often referred to as the jazz minor, as it's the mode most commonly used in jazz for minor compositions. Another way you can think of this scale is like a minor, but with a major 6th.

If we continue to 'invert' the original scale of C major we get the following modal scales.

· E - F - G - A - B - C - D	= **E PHRYGIAN** like a minor with a flat 2nd.
· F - G - A - B - C - D - E	= **F LYDIAN** like a major with a sharp 4th.
· G - A - B - C - D - E - F	= **G MIXOLYDIAN** like a major with a flat 7th.
· A - B - C - D - E - F - G	= **A ÆOLIAN** This is the natural minor scale.
· B - C - D - E - F - G - A	= **B LOCRIAN** Like a minor with both a flat 2nd and a flat 5th.

You will have noticed that the sixth mode IS the natural minor. All of the above modes share the same key signature - all natural notes. Of course all major keys can be inverted in this way. So, in the same way that a major key produces 7 chords, it also produces 7 related scales.

Getting back to the minor, you can now see why there is such a thing as a relative minor. Because it uses the same seven notes, and of course shares the same key signature as its relative major, there is a simple method for finding out the key signature of any minor key. You can either recall that the relative minor is the 6th inversion (mode) of the major scale and that therefore is a major 6th above the relative major, or a simpler way of doing the same thing is to invert the interval of a major 6th, which becomes a minor 3rd. A minor third on the bass is the distance between your 1st finger and your 4th finger. So, if you want to know the key signature of any minor key, place your 1st finger on the key note (if you want to know the key signature of A minor - place your 1st finger on A) then look at what note your 4th finger lands on, this will be the key note of the relative major (C major), therefore the key signature of A minor is the same as C major = All Natural Notes.

This method will keep you out of trouble in an emergency and is fine to get you started, however, you now hopefully know your major keys instantly and you need the same facility for minor keys. So below I've listed the learning chart of minor key sequences so that you can learn them in a complete and positive way, as you did with the major key signatures.

Minor Key learning chart

A minor = ALL NATURAL NOTES

SHARP KEYS : E - B - F# - C# - G# - D# - A#
ACTUAL SHARPS : F# - C# - G# - D# - A# - E# - B# *

FLAT KEYS : D - G - C - F - Bb - Eb - Ab
ACTUAL FLATS : Bb - Eb - Ab - Dd - Gb - Cb - Fb *

(* These two sequences are of course the same as previously learned for major keys)

The dominant 7th chord in the minor key.

One thing most people notice when they play the minor scale, as described so far, is that it sounds incomplete. By this they mean that when the octave is reached it sounds like it should continue as it has not reached its conclusion. The major scale by comparison is totally conclusive when you reach the octave. The main reason for this is that the seventh note of the major scale (known as the leading tone) is a semitone from the octave. This interval of a semitone definitely helps the mind to realise that the octave is about to be reached. So we can conclude that without a leading tone (a semitone interval between the seventh note of the scale and the octave or key note) a scale and key feels and sounds incomplete.

When this idea is passed onto chords the absence of the leading tone really tells. Firstly, in a minor key, the I, IV and V chords are all now minor. This helps the music retain its (usually) melancholic flavour but prevents the I chord from sounding strong. This then makes it more difficult to create tension and release because there is no obvious release point to work around. So, where does the leading tone come into chords?

In the major key, notice that the V chord naturally contains the leading tone for the key as the third of the chord. If we translate into the key of C major, the V chord is G major, the 3rd of G major is B, which of course is the 7th note, or leading tone in C major. The presence of this note is highly relevant in giving the chord progression V - I (G major - C major) such strength and authority.

When we move to the minor key, lets translate to the relative minor, A minor for now the V chord is, naturally E minor. E minor contains E - G - B. The leading tone to A is of course G#. Notice if you play the progression E minor to A minor, how inconclusive this is, you don't get the feeling that A is the strong chord or key note (unlike the progression G major - C major in the relative major key). However, if you substitute G with G#, playing the progression E major - A minor then the strength that was lacking with Em to Am is now apparent and A minor sounds strong.

The dominant 7th chord. The word dominant in music describes the 5th note of the scale. So the dominant chord is therefore the V chord. Composers throughout time have found that by adding the 7th to the V chord, its powers are greatly enhanced. This is why you very often find that a progression V - I is nearly always V7 - I. This is as true in the minor as in the major. The only added significance when you see V7 - I in the minor key is that it confirms, both by sound and sight, that you are indeed in a minor key.

The addition of the leading tone to the minor key also gives rise to a common scale called the harmonic minor scale. [see technique - target 5)

TARGET 5
PLAYING & READING

Bassline 17

Quite a lot to get to grips with in this one. Slides, solo introduction, every kind of repeat sign and sixteenth notes. As sixteenth notes are new to this target, you must refer back to your rhythm practise chart and thoroughly prepare these rhythms.

Repeat signs.

The commonest repeat is the 'bracket', which is easily identified because the outer line is heavy with a thin inner line and two dots positioned around the centre line of the staff. Usually this means repeat everything within the bracket once. However, an arranger can indicate several repeats by simply informing you x5 for example. Another complication is that these sort of repeats often include what is called a 'first time bar'. In bassline 17 this is quite straightforward, you play the bar with the 1. Bracket the first time through and then skip this bar on the repeat and play the 2nd time bar instead, continuing with the rest of the piece. It can be more complicated than this though, sometimes the first time bar will in fact be several bars. In this situation the 1st time bar bracket will extend across the whole of the 1st time 'bar' section. Another complication is that you may be instructed to play x5 or five repeats, in which case the 1st time bar should be marked 1.2.3.4 and the 2nd time bar 5.

The other way of creating repeats, usually used for repeating whole song structures, such as a whole verse and chorus, is the sign symbol 𝄋 . This sign is usually placed fairly near the beginning of a piece, often after the introduction, as in bassline 17. The instruction to "go back to the sign" will come, usually, near the end of the piece and reads "D.S". Often this is accompanied by a further instruction (as in bassline 17) 'al Coda', which means that when you repeat back to the sign you must look out for the 'Coda' symbol ⊕, this symbol instructs you to 'jump' to the coda. The coda will be the ending of the piece. However, it can still be tricky to find, if the coda section is long. In some songs the coda might be more than a page long. So if you're sight reading, it helps to be prepared - locate all the repeat symbols.

Bassline 17 should total 35 bars. (Don't forget that on return to the sign you still follow the bracket repeat instructions unless there is a note to the contrary.)

The overall feel of this piece is "laid back". The best approach to try and achieve this is to bring your emotions into the playing. You must be relaxed and find everything about the piece easy. This may take quite a bit of practise just to be technically and rhythmically in control. Try and picture a relaxing scene in your mind and concentrate on this image. You may not feel entirely comfortable with this concept yet, but the point to remember about creating feel when playing music is that the technical elements that bring this feel about, such as subtle adjustments to the timing and to the striking of the strings are usually much too small to consciously either count or control. Because of this the only way to ensure that the playing is affected in the right way is to manipulate your emotions, and let the emotions affect the way you strike and time notes. Of course this won't happen unless you've been practising and experimenting with all of the techniques associated with tone and dynamics.

Example

BASSLINE 17

Reading: dealing with longer pieces.

If you've been thorough with your studies thus far you should be ready to add to your careful studies some 'real' reading. Virtually any written music will do if its in the bass clef. The main aim of doing this is to get used to the fact that playing anything real, as opposed to exercises, puts you under more pressure. Also you will rarely find that everything is neatly in C major, or stays in C and although I will be giving you ideas on increasing your knowledge and ability in other keys, it will do you nothing but good to expose yourself to the real world from now on. Obviously, at this stage don't try and read music that is clearly much too hard, but do pick music that rhythmically does not go beyond eighth notes and that looks like the range of notes isn't too wild. Both these points should be immediately obvious at first sight.

Your goal when sight reading is, as has already been mentioned, to finish what you start - with no time keeping errors. If you have this attitude when reading then you will not fear music that is a little bit too hard for you.

Looking ahead.

Now that you're beginning to think about playing real bass lines and longer pieces, the ability to look ahead is essential. It requires real mental discipline to learn how to do this, but you will find it happens partly as a consequence of seeing more and more sections of notes as longer blocks. Obviously if you recognise a whole bar as an ascending scale of eighth notes, you can look straight away at the next bar while your hands automatically play this scale bar. The difficulty arises because you don't often have it handed to you on a plate quite like this, but you should by now appreciate the point. The later targets deal more and more with the recognition of blocks of notes. However, from now on try and force your eyes to look a bar ahead of what you're playing. In addition try and scan ahead looking for all the points that you observed during your brief preparation - this preparation is outlined in the following paragraphs.

What to look for before you begin to play:

You must prepare yourself for any music that you are going to sight read. Even if you are gigging or doing session work where there seems to be little preparation time, you must make a few basic checks.

1. Check the clef (not all bass music uses bass clef all the way through)

2. Check the Key signature.

3. Check the Time signature.

4. Check the Tempo (This will usually be in Beats per minute often marked showing the tempo of the quarter note (assuming the ¼ note is the beat) e.g. ♩ = 104. It is not a good idea to mark Beats per minute as 104 B.P.M. because sometimes arrangers use B.P.M. to mean Bars per minute. Fortunately this is usually obvious as it will be a low number such as 26 BPM (usually between 15 and 40 which are most unlikely ever to relate to beats per minute). To translate bar to beats per minute in 4/4 time multiply (in this example - 26) by 4.

5. Check the start and end and look for obvious signs of a key (or dominating note) so that the key centre and therefore name of key is definite. (This is relevant because your fingering, and probably more important, your expectations of the music will enable you to anticipate and react more effectively.)

6. Look for the highest and lowest notes throughout the piece. If the piece is long and the range of notes exceeds one position on your bass (11 notes on a 4 string bass) see if you can quickly spot the sections - range wise.

7. From the above - determine your hand position(s).

8. Look for changes to the Clef and/or Key signature. (If possible mark them.)

9. Check for repeats. Start by looking for use of the sign 𝄋. This can be determined usually by looking near the end for the D.S. al coda message. If you see this or just D.S. then the sign is likely to be near the beginning, after any intro's etc. If the instruction near the end was D.S. al Coda then you next need to find the Coda sign ⊕. Make sure also that you have checked where the coda begins. (obviously the coda will be at the end, but sometimes it can be quite long, taking a page or more.) Next look for the bracket repeats- ‖:‖ and make a note mentally (or highlight on the music itself) as to how many repeats are asked for and whether or not there is a second time bar to take into account.

Sight reading Bassline 17

Your first reaction to attempting bassline 17 for sight reading purposes is to think "forget it". I'm not ready for half of what's happening there. Your reaction would be totally correct. However, you can use this bassline to prepare yourself for dealing with more demanding sight reading situations. To sight read bassline 17 first time without errors would be quite an achievement. This though is not expected and is not the point of the exercise. What you need to develop is a technique for 'getting through' the piece in such a way that the audience would not be able to tell that you were only playing 50-60% correctly. You should not be too disappointed if you are unable to go from start to finish, even allowing for a lot of mistakes, when you first attempt this line as a sight reading exercise. Remember, this piece is the vehicle for you to learn a lot of important lessons, so keep trying and add new exercises to your practise repertoire. When you can survive on this piece, you will probably find that you have the confidence to attempt almost any piece, standing a good chance of getting from start to finish with the main groove and structure of the song delivered.

I am not recommending that you develop a technique for botching the job for evermore but am giving you the means to survive in a gig. If you have the confidence to sight read live, then your skills will advance very much more quickly than if you try and work up to a professional standard from the comfort of your living room.

To attempt to sight read bassline 17 with your current knowledge, you must first observe all the points mentioned in the above, "what to look for before you begin to play", section. Then you need to assess what is not realistic for you to attempt. Don't worry on this occasion if this seems like most of the piece.

At your current level the most immediate problems are:

1. An unfamiliar key; G minor (2 flats)

2. sixteenth notes

3. new intervals

4. repeat signs

Repeat signs of course need to be learned before you can seriously hope to play this piece from start to finish, with any hope of keeping your place. However, all musicians need to have studied the repeat structure before beginning to play, this structure is then memorised so that finding the sign and coda and playing the correct number of repeats etc. happens automatically.

The 3rd

The 3rd is a more difficult interval to deal with because it changes from being major to minor. The only way you know which is which is to know where you are in the key. Physically this should look after itself if you are reading in a key that you know properly. By now you should be pretty good at C major and therefore if you are reading E to G it is easy and logical for your fingers to find G without having to consciously think where G is. What you need to practice though, position by position, is playing 3rd's from every note. It is important that your fingers instinctively find the correct 3rd from any note for the key you're in.

Genuine improvisation methods - breaking the ice

Up till now you've developed skills needed to cope with chords, keys and getting round your instrument. By mixing up all of the exercises used to develop this skill a form of improvisation has been taking place. This improvisation has been controlled, you have understood why you've played every note, you have probably known what it would sound like before you actually played it, in other words each bar is so well known that you've learned the sound as well as the shape and individual notes that make it up. You will have added to this pre-composed bars with real melodic intrigue that you have memorised. You will also, when improvising on a G blues play differently every time. Make no mistake, you are improvising when you do this, however, it is not genuinely spontaneous. It is really spontaneity that enables a real creative process to begin. It is handled sub-consciously and so learning the basics has been essential grounding. Now you have to learn to cross the threshold between 'technical improvisation' and creative improvisation. This is quite a difficult step. It is also a step where you are on your own. I can try and push you in the right direction but you have to force yourself over the edge.

One barrier that people create for themselves is that they start off trying to improvise something absolutely amazing. Initially concentrate on finding a way of genuine spontaneous composition by keeping things really simple. For a start, if you are improvising on the first bar of a G blues, about to play G7 - C7, have you ever played G, G, G, B, C. The construction of this idea is so simple that you have probably considered it beneath your abilities so far. But the lesson is in the construction and the ease of memorising this construction. Root, root, root 3rd (provided it's the leading tone of next chord) - easy. How about Root, 5th, root, leading tone. The point about these simple examples is that they can easily be adapted for any position, any key any musical situation. Plus, remembering the construction of a bar, and the type of sound associated with this construction, (as I mentioned in Target 4, reflect and link writing procedure 8.) is one of the best techniques for helping you cross the threshold between technical and creative improvisation.

Composition

Chord/scale relationship

There is always a relationship between the chord being played and the scale that is associated with that chord. With some chords, the scale associated with them is always the same, but in most situations, and especially with simple triads the scale that can be associated with a given chord will depend on the key. Therefore before you can establish the chord/scale relationship you must determine the key of the music. Generally this means a key analysis. When you have your key signature, (the name of the key isn't so important) you can work out the scale. This is very easy.

You play from the root of the chord to the octave, using only notes that you have pre-determined through your key analysis.

In our song example this means that in key area 1 you can establish all of the scales to associate with the chords. A minor, play from A to A using only natural notes, (A natural minor scale). F major, play from F to F using only natural notes, (F Lydian scale). C major, play from C to C using only natural notes, (C major scale). G major, play from G to G using only natural notes (G mixolydian scale). It doesn't matter very much whether you know the names of the scales, what matters is to ensure you become familiar with the sound of the scale when played along with the chord. After all these seven notes will be the only notes you have to create your bassline.

To appreciate how these scales help, try and record the chords for the song and then play the scales as eighth notes in time with the chord changes.

To complete the song example, you first need to complete your Key Analysis. Before embarking on this make sure that you have completed Musicianship & Theory - target 5. Establishing the precise key of Key Area 1 (The Chorus) is quite easy. Remember it is not because you have two C major chords and an all natural note key that tells you the key is C major, (although these are clues) it is because C major is supported by F major and G major, the IV and V chords.

The verse is not in fact simply the VI and IV chords of C major as you might at first think. The E7 chord is part of the overall key of the verse. As you will have discovered in the M & T section, the minor key is often identified by the presence of a Dominant 7th chord returning to a minor I chord. Therefore the E7 chord, rather than being a specific key area is actually there to make A minor a distinct key centre in its own right, thereby establishing the key of the verse as A minor. Because the G# exists primarily to act as a leading tone to A it is best to approach the scale of this bar as if you are still in A minor (all natural notes) with an added G#. The scale you play over the E7 bar will be as follows: E - F - G# - A - B - C - D - (E). This may sound a bit odd at first, but it works. It is an inversion of A Harmonic minor (see technique-target 5). It is possible to incorporate the G# into all of the verse, however, this will give the whole verse the characteristic 'Turkish' sound which is probably not a good idea.

Beginning the creative process on the Model Song - The Concept

The most difficult stage of arranging a bassline for this song example is now complete, namely your chord list and key analysis. The actual creative part is quite a small part. Your aim is to establish a concept for the song. Try not to think of a concept as 'just a riff'. Your concept needs to, ultimately, take account of lyrics and the 'concept' of the song as a whole. So when developing your concept, even on this model song, try and invent a scene or image that you can base your choice of notes on. When working with a real song, finding notes and rhythms that suit the concept of the song idea, is what it's all about. Try not to fall into the trap of thinking that music is just a collection of notes. The notes are merely a vehicle for expressing an idea, or emotion of some kind. By ensuring that you always write music (basslines) from this perspective, you give yourself a good chance of remaining objective about music. In other words, its no good having a bassline that you've composed at home that's great fun to play, sounds amazing on its own, and trying to force that bassline onto a song with a concept that is totally unsuitable for that bassline. Always try and write 'fresh', once you understand the concept behind the composition or song. This requires confidence in your abilities. One reason why some musicians try to 'force' an inappropriate riff or musical idea onto a song, is that they lack confidence as composers.

The concept should not be any longer than 2 bars. 1 bar is perfectly acceptable. The problem with longer concepts is that they are likely to be too intrusive. If you imagine that your imaginary song is going to have a vocal line or other solo instrument then you must ensure that you don't overpower this top line.

One of your most important attitudes when arranging a bassline is to be really objective about whether the bass line contributes to the success of the top line. You must support unobtrusively. This does not mean that the bassline has to be dull, although many bass lines do 'play safe' for a variety of reasons. Obviously for the purpose of this exercise, even if you have managed to record the chords to a simple drum beat, I would not expect you to put a vocal line to it. This would not be necessary yet anyway, the point is keep the concept to two bars maximum and you will then establish a bass groove which can be interesting and demanding of you as the bass player, without demanding the attention of the listener, who should be listening to the vocals.

Because your actual creative input is only going to be about 2 bars (don't take this too literally - but your concept is your main compositional idea) you need to make sure it is good. How many inexperienced bass players have been happy to play the first thing that came into their heads simply because it got the job done. Most people can only think of one idea that fits. You should always aim to have about 15 ideas for any song that you write a bass line to. Most experienced players would be able to think of countless possibilities for any given situation. As a professional you may well have to invent a bassline instantly, only to be asked a couple of minutes later to try something else. This may happen a number of times before everyone is happy. The only way to give yourself this sort of ability at an early stage is to always aim for at least 15 ideas (concepts) for any song you arrange a bass line for.

It is obviously not possible for me to show you how to become a creative person, however I can try and encourage you to look for ideas. Often by working on one approach for ideas, another idea appears seemilgly out of nowhere. The point about creativity is that it doesn't always come easily or naturally. If you practice inventing basslines on a regular basis then you will become good at it.

With the song example, try establishing an idea around the A minor. Especially if you now have a tape of the chords you will have more time, as well as a genuine two bar section to try out your ideas. If you have no tape then you'll have to be a bit more careful, sticking a little bit closer to the 'rules' established in reflect and link writing and explored in your experiments. This is not a big disadvantage, as it is very rare that extremes work. Remember that basic 'rules' such as putting the root on beat 1 and having at least one more note from the chord in the bar work because they support the composition. If you push the boundaries of these rules then you run the risk of changing the composition. This may be acceptable if it is your, or your own band's composition but not at all acceptable if you're working for someone else or even doing a cover of an established song.

So how am I going to get you to create an imaginative concept from the pages of a book? Well, go back to your first target period when you were experimenting with the pentatonic scale, trying to come up with your first riff. Look for combinations of 3 perhaps 4 notes. To get a variety of ideas, ensure that your second note is always different. Bear in mind the 'rules' of reflect and link, although don't feel that you have to stick to them 100%. Hopefully, by now you will find it a lot easier to combine notes into sounds and patterns that you like the sound of so you may not need to force your creativity. However, to achieve the target of 15 ideas it may be helpful to introduce a few artificial measures.

Rhythmic variety and interest is hard at first. Usually the problem with ideas is just lack of experience. So, when lack of experience is to blame, put on a record and borrow some rhythms - don't worry the writers won't recognise them when you've imposed them on your note choices (They've copied them from someone else anyway). Other points to remember to help with rhythmic variety are that if you've come up with 3 or 4 concepts and they are all full of notes, go to the other extreme and come up with ideas that are have lots of rests. Try rhythms that stop and start. On two bar concepts how about a fairly full first bar followed by a sparse second bar. Don't be afraid of simple ideas, such as constant eighth notes, after all there must be thousands of hits that unashamedly have pumping eighth notes in the bass. Listen to styles of music that you wouldn't normally listen to. It's amazing how inspirational different types of music can be, especially if you're listening for ideas to borrow. One way or another there is a lot of music out there for you to listen to and get ideas from. Never think of this as stealing, we always learn from others whether we do so consciously or not.

The Model Song - solo

It is beyond the scope of this book to deal with the art of soloing. However, I would like to give you a fairly simple, reliable method of achieving a good solo.

The first point you need to realise is that as a bass player everything you've taken in up till now has been based around the idea that you play the root on beat 1 (or more precisely when the chord changes - usually on beat 1). When soloing the root is being played elsewhere (by the bass player usually) so it can be more or less ignored. However, the harmony of the composition should not be ignored. A good soloist puts as much effort into maintaining the harmonic progression as you would do as a bass player. The soloist does this by choosing the notes that occur on the chord change (usually beat 1) with great care. The main process of developing soloing technique is practising this skill.

However, as this solo idea is not strictly about how to improvise a solo we can skip the basics. You have the idea now that the note placed on the chord change is of great importance. The most useful note for the soloist is the 3rd and 7th (if present). These notes, when combined with the bass player's root, will give a full representation of the harmony or chord. (If you wish to develop your ability to improvise solos then begin by ensuring that you have the mental discipline to play either the 3rd or 7th of the chord on beat 1 (or with the chord change). Although the 3rd and 7th will be the safest, most correct notes to use as the 'backbone' of the solo, you can really consider any note in the key. The root is best avoided but can be considered. It is usually avoided because it creates a rather flat dull sound, useful if you want to slow the pace of the solo.

The start of your solo is to create the right 'backbone' for it. The backbone will be made up of one note per bar, or chord change, this note being the harmonically important note for the bar. Your aim is to find notes, that when played with the chords create the right overall atmosphere.

Example

A good method for achieving 'backbones' that make musical sense is to think of simple shapes and follow the shape when trying to choose notes. This is a bit hit and miss, but you usually find that if you try and keep the notes sensible (a large proportion of notes in the chord, 3rd and 7th especially) then this will work quite well.

Example

When you have a backbone that has the right kind of feel and atmosphere, you then need a melodic idea. This melodic idea will only need to be one or perhaps two bars long. Normally in a song the melody ideas used by soloists should refer to, or be influenced by the main melodies in the song. For this song example there is no melody to follow, so you can take the opportunity of using any melody that you can come up with. (If you find this hard refer to other Improvisation & Compositions sections of the book where I have suggested methods by which your creativity can be encouraged.)

As with all compositional ideas don't be satisfied with just one idea, really try to have several melodies to try.

Example

Unrefined solo ideas (i.e. melody ideas superimposed on 'backbones').

Pitch - Chromatic scale singing plus the major 6th and 7th.

Your pitch recognition should by now be quite good. The chromatic scale introduces an interesting twist. Learning to sing a chromatic scale will give you complete mastery of the semitone. Singing semitones accurately is not easy, but if you bear in mind that the semitone is the smallest increment of pitch, it is a very important sound to know and know well. Add the major 6th and 7th to your interval list. Remember there is no rush, do the 6th first and when comfortable add the 7th.

Rhythm - introducing the 16th note patterns and the counting method for 1/16th's

Sixteenth notes are for most bass players the rhythmic element that will provide the most fun. You should try and be patient though and only proceed with sixteenths if you're eighth notes are totally sound. Dealing with sixteenths is more difficult, and the variations that are possible increase dramatically.

Busking all the common major progressions.

II - V - I   Minor, major (or dominant 7th) major - final sounding I chord.

I - VI - IV - V   Major, minor, major, major (or dominant 7th).

I - VI - II - V   Major, minor, minor, major (or dominant 7th).

Sing your arpeggios through these progressions. Also try and play them or get a guitarist to play them. Playing root notes (only) will also help. There is so much music that uses these progressions you should try and find examples. Be careful here that the progression may only form part of the song. The chord type is very important to notice and learn. Very often when a you can hear a major, minor, major, major (or dominant 7th) you can deduce that the chord progression is I - VI - IV - V.

> *John Patitucci; one of bass's true virtuoso players. Usually seen playing six string bass he is capable of the most incredible solos and yet can really groove. He has released several solo albums to date and is also well known for his work with Chick Corea's Elektric Band. His videos are also some of the better tuition videos on the market.*

Review of technique through use of slow practise.

Throughout your study of technique (and indeed all aspects of learning bass) I have been pleading with you to take each exercise slowly. I am now going to show you how, through slowing it down to extremely slow, you can develop your technique still further - and if you're trying to learn to play faster, speed begins here - playing ULTRA SLOW.

All the exercises that I've introduced in this book and any that I'm yet to introduce will all benefit from ULTRA SLOW practise. The aim is to slow your technique down to such an extent that you can watch, and be conscious of every detail and aspect of that technique. If you're not convinced that this form of practise is going to work, then just try it on one simple exercise - the Major scale.

Initially it will be enough to work on the ascending part of this scale. There is no need to strain when playing ultra slow, so play D or E major, beginning on the A string so that the hand is comfortable. Firstly just contemplate what has to be achieved; you are about to play 8 notes across three different strings, you will use all of your fingers at some time or another. The right hand will, on an ascending scale, play by alternating the middle and index fingers without any exceptions. You are aiming for a smooth sound - no break between notes and you ultimately want to play the scale outrageously fast to impress all your friends. Your biggest enemy in playing fast is that your hand has so far been 'thinking' too slowly. In other words you've not been anticipating future actions far enough in advance. Don't worry about setting a tempo here, the speed you play will be determined by taking in all the aspects of technique, in both hands, for every note - a few seconds per note probably. Place your hand in the starting position. Firstly you need to check that the position of both hands is perfect. Your 2nd finger should be ready to play the first note of the scale. Before you play, where is your 1st finger. It should be waiting on or just above the 4th fret on the D string. Obviously, if you're going to check that the third note in the scale is ready and waiting then the second note is even more important. The 4th finger should be hovering just above the fret. Ideally this 4th finger should be no further than ¼ inch away from the point where it will eventually make contact with the string. If it is further away then don't worry for now, but you need to improve your control of the inactive fingers before you can expect fireworks from the fingers. So you are hopefully ready to begin playing, having prepared the first three notes of the scale. You will also be getting the idea about just how much there is to think about when playing the simplest exercise. Play the first note of the scale - as you strike the string look at how your right hand executes this procedure. Has it travelled directly through the string so that it now rests against the E string. Did the sound have attack? You can make fine adjustments to the attack by varying the rigidity of your right hand finger joints. Focus your attention back on the left hand. Keeping your 2nd finger held down with the correct (minimal) pressure to sustain the first note of the scale, begin to steer the 4th finger to its note. The action of putting the finger down should be smooth, at very slow speeds there will be a slight break in the sound, although it should only be slight. As the 4th finger makes contact, play the note with the right hand - again try and glance at the right hand to check its poise and balance. As soon as the second note of the scale is sounding the 2nd finger becomes free and needs to start, slowly, to head towards its next position, 5th fret of the D string. There must be no jerky movements when playing ultra slow, so although the 2nd finger needs to immediately make a move to its next position you should time it so that it arrives over the note at about the same time you play the 3rd note of the scale. Of course as you play the third note of the scale the 4th finger becomes free and starts its journey to the 7th fret of the D string. When the 4th finger leaves the A string, your hand is now free of this string. However, it should not jump into position suddenly, you should have been anticipating that your hand would eventually move completely onto the D string and have been slowly moving the whole arm so that as you play the third note of the scale your arm is already in position. The arm movement does not of course rest here but continues a slow progression towards its final position - playing the G string. The same anticipation is required of the right hand. You need to average out the movement that will be gone through from the beginning position to the final position.

If the above is not detailed enough for you then you should also take notice of any tics and shakes in the fingers and hands and try to exercise some control if at all possible. Often tremors and shakes in the fingers can be overcome simply by being made aware of their existence. The idea of playing ultra slow and analysing your technique to this extent may not appeal to everyone, but try and practise in this way, if only on the major scale 2 or 3 times a week. After a month or so, you should notice considerable improvement, and your understanding of how your hand works and the problems that are unique to you will enable you to solve technical problems much more easily as well as the ability to develop your own exercises to overcome specific problems.

Modal scales for variations in finger patterns.

For the moment I introduce modal scales purely as a technical alternative to major, minor and pentatonic scales.

Example

Slap - left hand percussive techniques

One of the most useful tricks to incorporate into the slap style are percussive, dead notes, produced by the left hand alone. Essentially this means 'hitting' the strings with the fingers held flat. As with hammer-ons and lift-offs this technique can give the impression of very fast playing because the left hand has time to 'hit' the strings in between either two thumb strikes or between the thumb and popping finger. It further increases the drum-like interplay that is possible with the left and right hands. There is a very definite knack to achieving a good sound with this technique. Most bass players would use all the fingers acting together to 'hit' the strings. It is better though, to keep the first finger gently resting on the unused strings to minimise harmonic ring and other unwanted noises. This leaves 2nd, 3rd and 4th to collectively hit or tap briskly onto the strings. It is best to aim for one string (usually the E string) to tap onto. The aim is to achieve a percussive note so it shouldn't matter if you hit the other strings as well. Some bass players intentionally hit all four strings together when using this technique. This can help to give more of a thump to the sound, especially at volume.

In isolation, hitting the strings across the fingerboard with the left hand does not obviously create a usable sound. This is because, as with dead or percussive notes created by damping the strings with the left hand while the fingers or thumb of the right hand strike the strings, left hand percussive notes need to be mixed in with pitched notes. It is also a style that comes into its own when the tempo is quite fast and the playing very fast.

The exercises for developing this technique do not necessarily produce good sounding exercises, especially when practising slowly, as you must do at first. Try and develop the ability to hit the strings snappily, ensuring that the fingers bounce off the string. If the fingers hit the string and stay firm on the string, the likely result is that a note or notes will sound, and because you will be hitting with the fingers held flat, you probably won't get a very nice sounding note either. Hit the string(s) hard and quickly, bouncing off the string to the point where the string is damped automatically. When practising exercises a degree of harmonic ring is inevitable so ignore this on exercises where the hitting of the string is regular and repetitive. However, you should ensure that you can create a clean unpitched 'note' if the exercise is paused after each strike (automatic damp).

Notice that all that is needed to notate this technique is to use a slur, or hammer on sign, because this indicates that the right hand plays no part in the execution of the percussive note.

Example

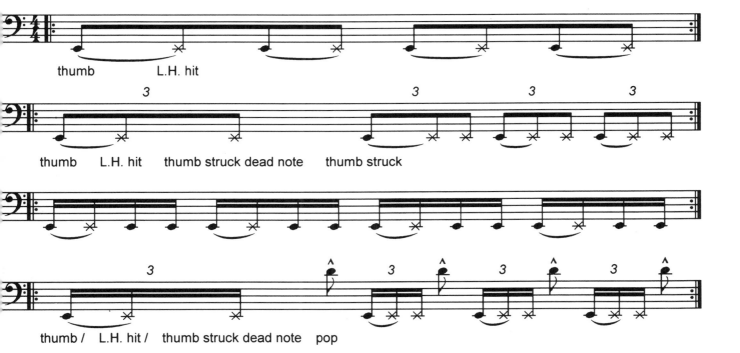

Common chord progressions (minor).

The common chord progressions in the minor key are:

- **I - VII - VI - V7**
- **I - IV - VII - III - VI - II - V7**

Learn these progressions by heart and then refer to Ear training sections to develop your aural understanding.

Inversions:

All chords can be inverted. Simply put, an inversion is achieved by re-arranging the notes of a chord. However, the note that determines the kind of inversion is the bass note. For example:

C - E - G = triad of C major in ROOT position
E - G - C = triad of C major in the 1ST INVERSION
G - C - E = triad of C major in the 2ND INVERSION

In each case it doesn't matter how the two higher notes are arranged so for example G - E - C = triad of C major in the 2nd Inversion, because G is still the lowest note.

Practically speaking, inversions create quite distinctive sounds compared to the more familiar sounding root position chords. To hear the effect properly try and get someone to play some chords on the guitar or piano and listen to how varying the bass note from root, 3rd and 5th affects the sound. They are valuable because unlike changing the chord itself, the same harmonic support is given to the melody line. The overall effect is different somehow, but it is quite subtle. A great exponent of inversions is Nathan East, especially noticeable when playing with Eric Clapton. I say especially noticeable when playing with Clapton because most of us are familiar with Clapton's material being played with the bass holding down the root. Nathan East seems always to look for a new angle to explore with the songs. He will also vary the inversions throughout a song's length, this has the effect of making the same chord progression sound fresh and different.

As well as changing the sound of the chord without affecting its harmonic responsibilities, inversions also give bass players and bass parts the opportunity of shaped lines. Playing in root position can sometimes mean that the bass note is darting all over the place when the music could do with a smooth scalar approach from the bass. A simple chord progression I - V - II - V or C major, G major, D minor, G major can illustrate this point (and other possibilities well). Instead of having to leap about playing from C to G to D to G, inversions give you the opportunity of playing a descending scale. C on the C chord (Root position), B on the first G chord (1st inversion), A on the D minor (2nd inversion) and G on the second G chord (Root position).

The above is designed to give you awareness of inversions. It is beyond the scope of this book to undertake a major study of the subject. However, experiment, so long as you listen to the effects inverting a chord has upon the chord and the song as a whole then you should be able to find uses for inversions.

Sight reading the fourth.

The fourth presents little difficulty physically as it always found at the same fret location on an adjacent string, however it is perhaps more difficult to spot in a crowd of notes. It differs from both the 3rd and the 5th in that it goes from a note on a line to a note on a space, or vice versa. The best advice for rapidly identifying 4th's is not to attempt them until you are absolutely sure about 5th's and also 3rd's, so don't rush the process.

Reading triads in close position. (Close position is when the notes of the triad are as close as possible, i.e. a 3rd apart. This as opposed to open chords where the intervals between each note might be first a 5th, followed by the 3rd of the chord a 6th above this (making it a 10th above the root)). Open position chords are not the subject of this book- you should be very happy if you can sight read close position chords.

Triads in Root position are the easiest to spot and deal with. Triads, as you know, are constructed in 3rd's, so therefore root position triads will be two successive 3rd's. This means either space - space - space, or line - line - line. Look at the example, it's easy to see but playing is not quite so simple. You have to appreciate where you are in the key, because like all 3rd's you cannot instantly see whether the chord is major or minor, only by understanding that the triad is built on a certain degree of the scale and therefore will be major or minor according to its' location. Again your knowledge and confidence of a position and where the correct notes are should make the fingers fairly instinctive about where to play. However, research all the root position triads in each position, in 2nd position (C major) you can play a triad of G (the V chord and therefore major), the common triad shape, 2nd finger on the root, 1st finger on the 3rd (next string) and 4th finger on the 5th. You can play A (VI chord, therefore minor), fingers as shown in example. B, which is the VII chord and therefore diminished. C, which is the I chord, and of course major. D, which is the II chord, minor. D, the III chord, minor. F the IV chord, major. If all this information is difficult to understand then revise the Musicianship and Theory sections. Knowledge helps, you can get away with recognising the block of 2 successive 3rd's, your fingers instinctively finding their notes because you know the position, but really understanding it makes it even easier. You gain a lot of confidence while you play if the music makes sense, because it will seem that bit more familiar.

Root position triads plus the octave. This block of 4 notes is easy to see. It is also quite easy and natural to play, but research as above.

1st inversion chords. More difficult to spot at first. They start with a 3rd and the second interval is a 4th. It is less common for inverted chords to go to the octave so it is sufficient to concentrate just on triads with inversions.

2nd inversion chords. Start with the 4th followed by the 3rd. Slightly easier, I think, than the 1st inversion to spot.

Just to really make the point, all of the above, are described as blocks, because you must avoid thinking about the individual notes that make them up, recognise the block and your knowledge and instinct will play the block whilst you get on with looking forward to the next group of notes.

Example

2 view of the perfect 4th

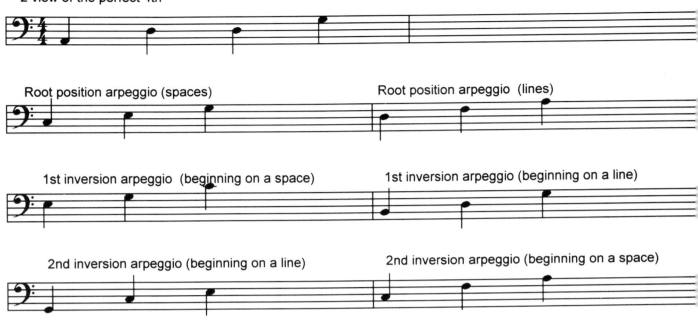

Root position arpeggio (spaces)

Root position arpeggio (lines)

1st inversion arpeggio (beginning on a space)

1st inversion arpeggio (beginning on a line)

2nd inversion arpeggio (beginning on a line)

2nd inversion arpeggio (beginning on a space)

Rhythm - The addition of rests and ties to the exercise structure.

To progressively introduce the full range of rhythmic variation to your studies, you need to incorporate ties and rests. Rests in particular can seemingly complicate a rhythm. The trick is to recognise which basic rhythms were the origin of the complex variation. The purpose of dividing your study into 18 patterns is so that you gain total confidence in all basic patterns and so recognise the origins of some possibly very complex rhythms.

The following examples show you how to gradually add ties to your rhythm exercises and then how to replace, bit by bit these tied notes with rests.

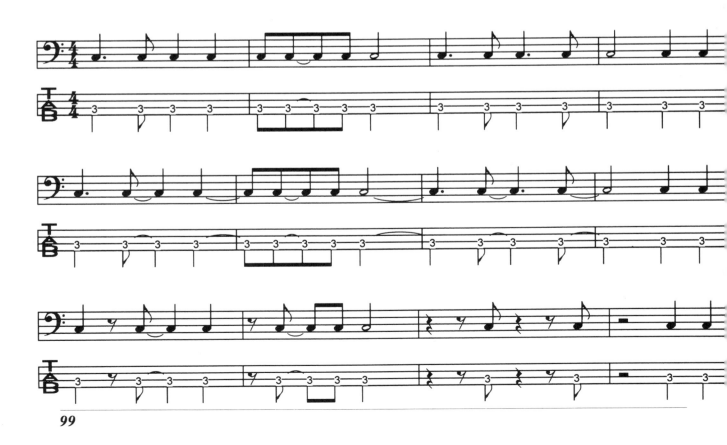

BASSLINE 18

The Model Song - developing the concept

By now you should have complete understanding of all the technical issues in the song example. You should also have at least 15 concepts. Initially choose your favourite concept for development. You may decide later that although your favourite idea worked well when repeated on the same chord or root that it doesn't sound so good when threaded through the whole song. So don't discard your other ideas yet.

Developing a concept is quite simple. At first, you simply transfer your concept or riff from one chord location to another. This means that you will transpose the original idea. The only difference between this and moving the riff from one chord to another in a 12 bar song is that in our song example, and typically in most songs there are mixtures of major and minor chords. In addition to having to deal with different chord types there is the key to work to and the range of chords may mean that you have to take care which root you choose so that you don't run out of notes.

The aim of the 1st development is to impose your concept onto each chord location. Don't worry that this may sound awkward, the important point for now is that the composition is disciplined. When transposing make sure that you stick to your decisions about the key. So when transposing within Key Area 1, all the notes will be natural, when transposing to Key Area 3, G is sharp. Provided you follow this then the only other point you need to watch is that each note of the original concept is transposed to the equivalent note for the new chord. For example if the original concept is made up of the root, 3rd and 7th then simply ensure that all other bars contain the relevant root, 3rd and 7th. That's all there is to it - for now.

Example

The Model Song - enhancing the concept and finishing the song.

You should now have all the main structures in place, a good concept running throughout the verses and choruses, and the main points of the solo (backbone and melody). Don't be too disappointed if it sounds a bit crude at the moment, there could well be notes that simply don't work at all. The reason for getting to this point is so that we have compositional discipline and integrity. This may sound very highbrow to read, but all it means is that the music is consistent to the listener. The problem that many inexperienced musicians face is that they have too many different ideas in the same song. To the listener this is just confusing, not imaginative. This is why the basic concept is so important - it will carry the whole song. In a real situation this concept needs to take into account the meaning of the song - lyric, the melody and of course the ideas of other musicians.

Now is the time to refine the ideas that you've had, bring them to life - but retain the discipline. It should be almost impossible to destroy the concept now that it's in place - so our composition is safe. When transposing a concept onto different chord locations problems can occur with certain notes. The main notes that suffer are the 3rd and 7th as these notes change their position, relative to the root, depending on whether the chord is major or minor. However, it doesn't necessarily follow that if you incorporate 3rd's or 7th's into your lines that these notes will not work when the chord type changes. On many occasions they work fine. The typical situation in which they don't work is where the character of the interval is integral to the whole idea. For example, if your concept is made by the minor quality of the minor third, you may not like it when the concept is transposed to a major chord and the 3rd has to become major. In addition there may be other notes that don't work, or that you just don't like.

There are a number of simple solutions for 'bad' notes. The first thing to try is to replace the 'bad' note with one note found either side of the offending note. If this doesn't work then try replacing the 'bad' note with a neutral note. A neutral note is one that is unaffected by major or minor changes, such as the fourth or fifth. If this still doesn't work, try replacing the 'bad' note with the root, either in its original location or as an octave. If you're still not satisfied then try replacing the note with a rest, or sustaining the previous note for longer, so missing out the offending note. Usually though the first suggestion, to simply move the note either up one, or down one, solves the problem.

Go through the entire song until you are happy that all the notes work. Notice that even if you've made quite a lot of adjustments that your original concept sounds untouched.

The next part of refinement is to look at the song as a whole. Approximately three minutes in which you must retain the interest and trust of the listener. You should now have a disciplined composition, so the listener will trust you but this is not enough always to keep the listener interested. The song needs to be a living structure, from the beginning it needs to grow and develop. The choruses need to stand out as the climax of each section of the song (usually), the middle 8 needs to be a departure from the original idea so that when the song returns it seems to have grown even more and once again sounds fresh.

From the above you know that the choruses need a little extra. This can be as basic as playing two eighth notes on the first beat (assuming that this is not already happening). If your concept starts with a quarter note or a longer sound this will create quite a strong push, and therefore increase the perceived excitement. If your original concept is quite busy, rhythmically, you may find that you have to consider cutting notes out of the original concept in the verse. Experiment with adding to the rhythm, especially on Chorus sections, and also see what cuts can be made without altering the sound drastically.

In addition to creating a difference in pace between the verses and choruses you need to structure the pace of the whole song. As a song develops, new ideas need to be introduced to the arrangement. In a real situation this role is shared by all of the musicians, but for now it is all down to you. The best approach is to start at the beginning and take the song section by section. I always break songs down into four bar sections, and treat these sections as building blocks, each block must be a logical development of the previous block and each block must, in some way, offer something new for the ear.

The Intro:

The job of the intro. is to first of all grab the attention of the listener and then to set up the style and groove of the song. There are many techniques that songwriters use for intro.'s but for now think what you can do within the limitations of this exercise. To attract the attention of the listener, you need something dramatic. A powerful counter rhythm is a good idea, such as playing root notes only on the 2nd and 4th beats. Try some high notes, perhaps in an eighth note rhythm for one or two bars before dropping down to your main bass line. You could try altering the inversion of the chords to create tension with a descending bass line, such as bar 1: C (root of C chord), bar 2: A (3rd of F chord, 1st inversion), bar 3: G (root of G chord), concluding on a very sinister sounding bar 4: E (3rd of C chord, 1st inversion). Or try holding C all the way through the intro., C (root of C chord), C (5th of F chord, 2nd inversion), even C under the G chord (high tension) concluding of course with C (root). If the C under G chord is a bit too much for your taste, try dropping down to B (1st inversion) instead. I hope that these suggestions help you experiment constructively and that they build into you a sense of just how important intro.'s are to a song.

The first verse.

 Your first consideration is how to get into the first verse, do you need to introduce the opening chord/note with a fill of some kind. A fill is basically a linking structure used usually between two sections of a song as opposed to a simple link which is the means by which each bar or chord is linked together. The construction of a fill is similar to a link and the ideas of scale link, leading tones 5th's etc. are the same. The basic difference is that a fill is usually longer and more involved than a link, often taking up a whole bar. The length of the fill depends upon its importance. A fill in to a chorus is likely to be a bar long because the chorus is the most important section of the song. A fill to the opening verse needs to be much more subtle, perhaps a couple of beats long at most with maybe three notes used. A good example of a fill to A minor from C major is to play low E on beat 3 of the preceding bar with G on beat 4 and G# on 4&. This can be made a little lighter by delaying the E until 3&. The construction of this fill is very logical, the E is both the 3rd of C major and more importantly the 5th of A minor, this subtly prepares the mind for the possibility of an A chord, the G - G# - A chromatic scale creates a smooth and simple introduction to the A chord. The 5th link often plays a big part in fills even if scales of some kind actually complete the fill. So fills are constructed usually with the same devices that you have used to create links, except that fills are usually made longer by combining these devices or by enhancing with rhythm and duplicated notes.

The first verse is 16 bars long and because of the length needs some thought. Never play your part mechanically or exactly the same throughout. It is true that in some really 'poppy' tunes bass lines are very rigid - and rightly so, but for now develop a lot of ideas that could be used if the development of the song is down to you. A good approach here is to trim the concept down for the first 8 bars, gradually allowing the full concept to return by the end of the verse.

The fill to the chorus. After such a long verse the first chorus is going to be very important. If a listener is made to wait for something then its going to have to be good. A substantial fill to the first chorus will help it succeed in making it sound important and exciting. Substantial does not necessarily mean complicated. A very effective fill is to play a simple scale from G to C. This can either ascend or descend. If descending, the easiest way to arrange the notes for the fill to take up the whole bar is to play each note twice, GG, FF, EE, DD to C on beat one of the Chorus. Ascending will require a chromatic scale to have a similar effect and treatment, GG, AA, A#A#, BB to C on beat one of chorus. The following are quite a lot of ideas for fills to the chorus. Try them all out, and then see if you can invent something of your own from what you've learned about constructing fills thus far. Also see Scale Formulae, later in this section. The chorus is able to take a small fill in the middle as it repeats although this is not essential.

Fill back to verse 2.

Ideally if you use a fill at this point in the song its function would be to try and slow the pace prior to the verse. A good trick for slowing the pace is to fill with 2 or 3 well chosen notes, and place these notes off the beat.

Verse 2:

Verse 2 is only 8 bars and, although you may have succeeded in slowing the pace a little with a neat fill, you will need to maintain the momentum that has now developed in the song. A small fill as the verse repeats, in addition to a more definite and repetitive groove than was perhaps the case in the first verse.

Fill to 2nd chorus.

This could repeat the fill used before the first chorus, however, bearing in mind the usefulness of giving the listener something new throughout the song it is probably better to have a new fill.

Chorus 2:

Not a lot of room for manoeuvre in this Chorus. Possibly the replacement of an off-beat eighth note with 2 sixteenth notes, or similar doubling of rhythm on a long note, quarter note to 2 eighth notes etc. Don't overdo this, just pick on one note to double and stick to it throughout the chorus.

Middle 8 solo.

So far you only have a 'backbone' and melody idea, the solo has not yet been crafted. As with your bassline concept, the melody is transposed onto each note of your 'backbone'. Do this literally at first, and don't worry if it is a little crude. Once again the idea behind this is to give you a fairly simple means of giving your solo shape and discipline. You can now cut out quite a lot of notes. A fairly good approach is to play for one bar and then relax, until you reach bar 6 when the solo needs to keep moving. You can also develop the melody a little without disturbing the original concept.

The easy tricks to employ here are:

1. Try altering the octaves of one or two notes

2. Extend the above idea so that the second time you play the melody (perhaps on bar 3) you 'invert' it. For example if the notes followed the following interval pattern, ascend a 3rd, ascend a fourth, descend a 2nd, then to invert this melody, subtract each interval from 9 and reverse the direction. The above melody would now follow an interval structure; descend a 6th, descend a 5th, ascend a 7th.

3. Invert only 1 or two selected notes.

All the above examples develop the melody by keeping to the same notes and changing the octave and/or direction of the notes. You can further enhance your solo in the same way that you can with the bassline by changing 'bad' notes and by adding fills.

A good place for a fill is;

1. During the last bar of the chorus preceding the middle 8, this is more of an introduction to the solo than a mere fill, however, the construction would be basically the same.
2. During bar 4 of the solo, to break the solo into two sections, the second of which is then more of a climax

3. During bar 8. There is a need for an important fill to take the solo back to the verse.
Remember that the E7 is key area 3 with G#, and that this key area is actually part of the verse key, A minor.

You can further enhance the solo by employing linking notes in the normal manner, although you can't use leading tones as such because the middle 8 is all one key, and the notes that make up your backbone are probably not the key note. Take care that you remain in key. Little scale runs and fifths are especially useful.

Verse 3:

This verse has been put in here to complete the middle 8 and conclude the solo. It will not last long, 8 bars is about 15 seconds, and your job is to try and make the first beat of the final chorus as powerful as possible. This will definitely involve creating a major fill in the 4th bar of this verse.

Final Choruses:

The song has reached its climax and your most important role here is to keep it as consistent as possible. The concept should now be kept to with no more additions required to the whole. Fills are still possible and when the chorus repeats for one final chorus the momentum needs to be maintained. If anything extra is possible then use it. There is scope during final choruses for the bass to introduce melodic fills, by shooting up into the high notes and playing an answer phrase to the vocal. Also extra fills during bars 2 and 4 are possible to really keep the pace developing.

The Model Song example shows some of the ideas described above in practice. The introduction uses a pop on beat one to grab the audiences attention and from then on plays an off beat rhythm that will relate quite closely to the 2nd bar of the two bar concept used in this example. The second half of the introduction incorporates inversions to heighten the tension. In the verse compare the original concept with the final bassline. The main changes have been forced on the F and E7 bars because of the (common) need to keep the notes as low as possible. Notice how insignificant these changes are to the overall sound and concept.

The chorus uses the idea of playing 2 eighth notes on beat one to increase the pace and makes some minor note adjustments. The 2nd verse has some additions to keep the pace up and uses a very simple, yet powerful fill into the 2nd chorus. Notice the fill into the solo, this is both compositionally sensible and also technically helps the hand to climb the neck in stages. The development of the solo is much more involved, although this mainly means leaving out a great many notes from the literal solo derived by combining a 'backbone' and melody together. If you look carefully there is nothing very intellectual about the solo development, the sixteenth note flurry is about the only real 'extra' in the solo. There is one major adjustment, the final bar has been completely moved from the note originally suggested by the 'backbone', simply because it didn't sound right being played from the B. The adjustment has been to the root in this case - not a major surprise. The only other development has been to return to the intro' idea for the final 'run out' chorus.

In addition to the technical adjustments that are needed to refine a bass part, there should always be room for spontaneity. This means that you can improvise within the structure you've composed. Again, if you improvise from a position of real discipline your spontaneous additions will enhance, rather than destroy your bassline. This form of improvisation should be really quite subtle, although you will need all of your improvising skills to achieve it. It can mean unique fills each time you play. Sometimes you may add more notes to the chorus rhythm to increase the pace than at other times. It may just mean a slide into a note that isn't normally there. The ability to bring a song to life through very subtle improvisation of a disciplined composition is the hallmark of all the great players. The whole idea of writing your bass lines in this way may seem a bit excessive, but keep in mind that the main weakness of the inexperienced bassline composer is that their parts are: 1. not objective, i.e. the concept of the bassline does not suit the concept of the song. 2. The concept (which is also heard as the overall groove remember) is difficult for the listener to define and therefore sounds confusing. So the point of the exercise is to be made  aware of the need for compositional discipline. Following this method will ensure that your compositional discipline is always present, and you'll find that by working on slight modifications you can end up with a bassline that is also very sophisticated, without sounding in any way complicated. You should consider not being noticed a compliment. If you can be objective and unobtrusive in your compositions yet at the same time be playing parts that are alive and full of interest and satisfaction for you to play then you have really cracked it.

John Paul Jones: One of the first true musician bass players. Famous for his work with Led Zeppelin, John Paul Jones was a truly awsome bass player. His true musicianship is fully realised on his improvised bass solo in the 'Lemon Song' on Led Zep' II. Not only is this a masterpiece of improvisation, the groove is perfect.

The Model Song

Example

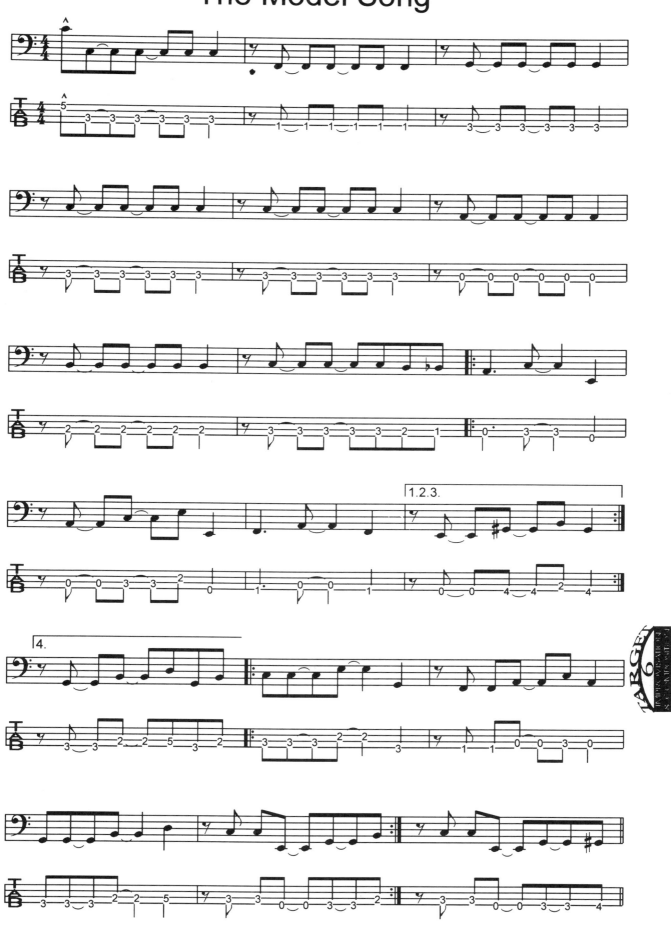

Example

107

The G blues - scale formulae

The idea behind scale formulae is to give you some quick and effective ways of constructing bars that are scalar, as opposed to triad based. One thing to bear in mind when using scales, especially when playing to four note 7th chords is that you are only ever a 3rd away from the next note in the chord. So in other words if you play a 3 note diatonic scale in any direction, starting on any note in the chord (usually this will be the root) you will automatically play a second note from the chord. This of course means that a scale of 3 notes will automatically reflect any chord (because you will have played at least 2 notes from the chord).

Although scale formulae are designed really as fall backs that don't need conscious thought for every note you play, when you are using them for improvisation development try and ensure that you are able to think of the notes that make them up.

The way to remember a scale formula and understand how they've been constructed is to learn the interval they relate to first. This interval is referring to the interval from the root of one bar to the root of the next bar. For example if you are playing G7 and going to C7 and you begin the G7 bar on low G, then the interval from this G to C is a perfect 4th. If you started on middle G then you would have a choice of descending to C which would be a perfect 5th or ascending to middle C which is a 4th. The following formulae are designed to help primarily with improvising the G blues, but all can be adapted to create fills and for improvising on more complex structures.

Scale Formulae

1. Interval of a 5th = Diatonic scale

2. Interval of a 4th = Chromatic scale

3. Unison (return to same note=Diatonic scale (either up 3 notes and down 1, or down 3 notes and back up 1 note). [see example]

4. Ascending Octave = Jump a 5th, then diatonic scale

5. Descending Octave =Descending diatonic scale / jump a 5th to next root.

6. Descending 2nd or ascending 7th (as in the D7 to C7 change in G blues) = Jump to the 5th of the chord and then ascend chromatically.

You should study the examples to see exactly what is meant by the above. Then use the above phrases as your means of remembering the formulae.

Create an exercise playing through the G blues using scale formulae on every bar. Keep strictly in an important hand position while doing this and view the exercise in the same light as the variable triad exercise, practising it in all the important hand positions.

Example

The G blues - putting it all together

If you've made it to this point with your brain still intact, then congratulations. You should now know where all the natural notes are on the bass. You should have a strong feeling for logical positions for your hand on the bass (important hand positions) and you should know every possible permutation for G7, C7 and D7 chords. You will actually now know three keys, ALL NATURAL NOTES, 1 SHARP AND 1 FLAT. (If you prefer, you now know - C major, G major, and F major.) You have several means of invention:

1. Basic Fall backs, which are the simplistic triad shapes played as close position arpeggios followed by a 4th beat link. 2. Variable triads; a full vocabulary of triad variation.

3. Many (I hope) original ideas created from the reflect and link writing exercise.

4. An ability to originate bars by thinking of structures that you know will work. E.g. root, octave, 5th leading tone.

5. Scale formulae

If you are confident that you really know the fingerboard, through use of important hand positions you should now think about loosening up a bit. Feel the hand flow from one position to another within the same bar if needed. Think about extending variable triads to allow for a greater range of notes than was possible within a single hand position. As your knowledge and confidence grows, gradually increase the tempo. However, exercises should always be done on the slow side, always think that exercises should be consciously controlled, unlike performance which should be sub-consciously controlled.

Listen to others:

The only way to practise this is when playing with other musicians. It is all too easy to isolate yourself by your own playing. You concentrate so much on what you're doing that you are completely unaware of what the musicians around you are doing. This is especially true if you have little experience of working within a musical group of any kind. Your long term aim is to develop your ear to such an extent that you can actually hear the notes and chords being played by others and react technically to what others are doing, as well as emotionally. However, even a relative beginner can react and respond to what other musicians do, simply by being disciplined and determined enough to really listen to others. It is beyond the scope of this book to get involved in how precisely to react to the musical ideas that other musicians bring to the improvisation session. To be truthful, there are no 'rules' about what exactly to play in response to others anyway. Think about listening on a simple level at first. Are the other musicians playing loudly or quietly, are they playing fast or slow. These are not difficult things to hear and respond to in a logical and musical fashion. Start with these simple goals and gradually, as your ear develops, take in more detail about what is going on around you.

Francis 'Rocco' Prestia;
Rocco is one of the all-time
most infuential bass players.
He is known for his work
with cult American funk
band 'Tower of Power'.
Rocco employs a finger-style
right hand playing that
seems to be almost
continuous 16th notes.
Listen to the energy and the
consistency of the groove.

TARGET 6
EAR TRAINING

Pitch - completion of all the basic intervals, learn the minor 6th and diminished 5th.

The method by which you can learn the sound of any interval should be well established by now. The above intervals, needed to complete all the interval sounds of less than one octave, can be learned at any time. Do ensure that all other intervals have been covered, and begin with the sixth as the dimished 5th is likely to be the least used of all your interval sounds.

Rhythm - Coping with 16th note patterns

In order to deal with any 16th note rhythm pattern, you must count in, and 'feel' 16th notes. The problem faced by most bass players when trying to perform a 16th note groove, is that they don't feel the 16th note groove the entire time. This is quite energetic. To begin with, when learning the basic 16th note patterns count **1 e & a 2 e & a 3 e & a 4 e & a**. Count loudly and energetically. Make sure, at first, that the counting is strictly equal.

Of course your first goal is to play the actual patterns found in the rhythm pattern list on page 44. Once you have grasped the basic patterns you need to appreciate swing. 16th notes are always swung when played by human beings. One reason why old fashioned type drum machines sound mechanical is because they do not introduce any element of swing into the beats and patterns. To swing 16th notes involves delaying the 2nd and 4th 16th note (the "e" and the "a"). This delay, or swing, can be subtle or very pronounced. Strictly speaking reggae is a slow 4/4 time with heavily swung 16th notes. Because of the degree of swing, reggae is often written in 12/8 time, however, trying to put a triple time feel onto reggae will result in a very stiff sound indeed. In addition to reggae, using a slightly faster beat is the music of James Brown, which is also heavily swung 16th notes.

In developing your ear for 16th notes never diminish the importance of counting out loud. You can practise swinging the 16th notes with your counting. Eventually you do not want to be counting any rhythm out loud, but by learning all your patterns with a strong count, when the time comes to count less verbally, you should find that you have a very powerful feeling for 16th notes.

Busking: The minor progressions

I - VII - VI - V7	Minor, Major, Major, Dominant 7th (unmistakable)
I - IV - VII - III - VI - II - V7	Minor, Minor, major, major, major, diminished, dominant 7th.

Notice how this common progression uses all seven chords found in the key. Once again the aim of this section is to learn by sound these progressions. Listen to them played simply and sing through them. When you can recognise them played simply listen to records and try and spot the chord progressions that you have learned. Try using your 'singing through the chords' technique when listening to see if it helps you identify other progressions.

Supplement

TECHNIQUE:

It is my profound hope that as a result of studying this book you now understand all the fundamental techniques for playing bass. Finger-style, slap and use of the pick have all been covered. Because this is a foundation course, the book does not contain pages and pages of ever more complex technique exercises. There are some books that explore the subject to total excess. By all means buy other books such as these to supplement this book, however, you should try to **evolve your own exercises**. You now have a good grounding in technique and should be able to evaluate the logic behind all techniques discussed, even if you haven't yet mastered them. If you have a problem caused by lack of technique, examine every aspect of playing in the area of concern. This basically involves playing ultra slow, so that you can look at your technique in great detail. From here you can usually see immediately where the problem stems from and it is usually quite a simple matter to invent an exercise to overcome the problem. Another 'skill' here is in being realistic about how long an exercise will take to achieve its objective. Many people get as far as evaluating a problem and inventing an exercise to deal with it only to be devastated that after only a few days the problem persists. Technical goals can sometimes take months, even if you are doing everything right, so be realistic and patient.

MUSICIANSHIP

This book has concentrated on quite basic issues; Fingerboard, Keys and Chord construction. What has been kept to a minimum is the exploration of the vast number of chords in existence. Chords are best learned in the context of a composition. When trying to increase your knowledge and experience of keys and chords in particular try and do this by learning AND ANALYSING real music. If you are in a band really explore the compositions working out the chords and keys and ensuring that this knowledge is retained for as long as you play that particular composition.

For key/fingerboard study you only have four sets of important hand positions to learn as each principal key is so similar to the two most closely related keys that they can be learned as minor modifications to the original key. Take the study of ALL NATURAL NOTES as a key signature. You now know all the important hand positions and hopefully are really confident about the location of ALL natural notes on the bass. The following examples show the minor modifications needed to learn the important hand positions for the key of 1 sharp and for 1 flat.

When you understand this and can easily get around the neck, using the G blues as your main vehicle, you should be able to learn the next set of 3 keys quite easily. You now know the system. It isn't essential that you adopt a blues as your vehicle for study, but again you know this system well and it will make the study of the key quite easy.

The principal keys are:

1. ALL NATURAL NOTES
2. 3 FLATS
3. 3 SHARPS
4. 6 FLATS   /   (6 SHARPS)
(physically the same, but mentally you would, of course, have an entirely new key - so arguably there are 5 principal keys. However, it is more common to work in 6 flats than in 6 sharps, so start with flats and then, if you need to, learn as 6 sharps using the same method.)

How quickly you try and learn all of your keys will depend on the kind of music you play and your overall ambition. If you want to be a working professional, you cannot have any weaknesses in any key - no excuses. If on the other hand you are basically playing rock in a local band, you may never need to know 6 flat keys etc. so concentrate on getting really good at the keys you encounter day in day out.

PLAYING AND READING:

You cannot expose yourself to enough music. The better you are at reading the easier you will find it to absorb a lot of music. Try and get hold of as much 'real' music as you can. The pieces in this book, whilst being carefully constructed to develop your playing, need to be augmented with genuine 'hit' basslines. Studying basslines that have been used on hit records makes the line that bit more authoritative compositionally. In further developing sight reading, progress logically and slowly. This book has, I hope, shown you how to build from very simple elements to the point where you can hopefully tackle 'real' basslines, often with 100% accuracy. Increasing your skill in sight reading is simply a matter of adding more elements, bit by bit.

IMPROVISATION AND COMPOSITION:

The scope of this book has been to enable you to see how improvising is achieved. To be capable of improvising over any and every possible composition means thorough knowledge of your keys and a lot of chords. Even then you must put in hour after hour of practice to develop, especially if you want to play jazz, which is usually characterised by its freedom and need for improvisation. It has not been my intention to show you how to play jazz in this book, however, if you apply what you have learned throughout both the Composition sections and Improvisation sections and develop your ability to improvise with real discipline and compositional integrity, then you are on your way to being able to play jazz.

Try and put as much time as possible into writing your bass lines and incorporate as much of the method used in this book as possible. As compositional discipline gradually becomes second nature, you can allow yourself to compose more and more sub-consciously.

EAR-TRAINING:

I hope I'm wrong, but I bet that this has been your least favourite subject. You need good practice discipline to progress and progress is often slow, but if when reading this you know that you've cut corners and are still not hearing musical sound clearly and quickly, revise the subject. Perhaps incorporate more 'real' music, and learn to sing tunes, analysing intervals and chords etc. Also practise singing tunes whilst playing the basslines that accompany them, or at the very least whilst holding down the root of the chords.

PRACTICE v. PERFORMANCE:

The art of practice is to consciously control every action. The art of performance is to sub-consciously control every action. To totally 'let go' and so become 'one' with your instrument, which is the ideal in performance, requires a great deal of confidence in your technical, rhythmical and musical skills. However, always strive for this ideal. If when trying to allow the sub-conscious to control things, errors occur then it really means that you've a gap in your knowledge, caused by lack of practice or cutting corners in practice.

LIVE PERFORMANCE TECHNIQUE:

Whatever your direction and whatever style of music you play, you are always playing to an audience. You are trying to entertain the audience, trying to communicate with them, expressing your own ideas and emotions. So, when performing live make sure that this is your objective. Make contact with the audience and don't let go. It's no good being shy about playing to an audience, although all musicians are affected by playing in front of people they must control negative emotions like fear in order to bring out the emotions intended to be communicated by the music.

One of the simplest tricks to help you conquer fear or nervousness when playing live is to practise playing all your basslines without once looking at your instrument. Concentrate on looking at the audience. If you condition yourself to always looking out at an audience, you'll soon realise that there is nothing to fear. The audience will think that you have no fear and will actually warm to you much more as a result. They will also respond positively to the fact that you are acknowledging their presence. No one likes watching a band where some or all of the musicians spend the entire show looking at each other or at their instruments. As you prepare for live performance, practise all your bass lines either looking slightly to the left and 'out' into the (imaginary) crowd, or looking right, or looking either hard left or right. You need to control your eyes, they must not flick from side to side, definitely they must not close for any length of time and your posture needs to support the direction you are looking in. When playing in front of a real audience, it is not a good idea to 'eyeball' specific people in the audience. Simply pick a point on a wall and fix your gaze on that spot, only changing your view to pick out another pre-determined point on the wall. To the audience, who don't know precisely what you're looking at the effect is a very confident performer that works to the audience all of the time. This technique is just as important for you, the bass player, as it is for the main front man or woman.

Bass strings. There are many different makes of bass string. However, the main points to know about strings are that they come in different finishes. Flat wound, half wound and roundwound. This finish drastically affects the sound. Flat wound have few overtones and therefore sound dull (useful for some kinds of studio playing). Roundwound are very bright, piano sounding strings, much liked by slap players in particular. Half wound are an attempt to give the benefits of flat wound, no overtones and no finger noise, with the bright tone of roundwounds. Like most compromises they don't entirely succeed in this goal.

In addition to finish there are different materials, such as nickel, steel and even gold plated strings. In practice there is little difference between materials.

Perhaps most important to bass players is the string gauge (thickness of each string). When starting out on bass always choose a standard gauge, which is likely to be identified as, for example .40 - .100. This gauge will give you the best compromise. Some bass players use a light G string, .35 and a heavy bass string, .105. This is known as a custom set. A lot of shops will sell strings individually enabling you to create your own custom gauge, if you are not happy with the standard sets available.

The Best of British: Some names of UK bass players to look out for:
Dill Katz
Paul Westwood
Julian Crampton
Laurence Cottle
Jack Bruce
Joe Hubbard (based in UK)
Michael Manring
Mo Foster
Percy Jones

notes:

notes:

notes: